TEST YOUR CREDIT MATHEMATICS 2001

by

P.W. Westwood,
Principal Teacher of Mathematics,
Kirkcaldy High School

and

C.M. Stewart

ISBN 0 7169 3255 5
© *Westwood & Stewart, 2001.*

ROBERT GIBSON · Publisher
17 Fitzroy Place, Glasgow, G3 7SF, Scotland, U.K.

INTRODUCTION

The purpose of this book is to provide practice which will develop essential mathematical skills — reinforcing knowledge of basic facts and promoting facility in handling appropriate mathematical processes.

Such practice should be regular, like an athlete's training, not excessive nor belatedly concentrated in a short space of time.

"Knowledge and Understanding" is the first assessable element in Standard Grade Mathematics. This covers the facts, concepts, skills and routine procedures required to carry out mathematical problem solving, as well as the appropriate use of mathematical notation and symbols. A candidate aiming at Credit level can fail through ignorance of, or weakness in, these basic items (or their application). This book, used as an extra to any main text, can help to make good such deficiencies.

Originally conceived as additional homework examples, the material contained in the book is designed to be used at the rate of one set of examples each night, five days a week, during the fifteen weeks leading up to the examination.

The final exam has a paper where a calculator is available and another where it is not. Exam questions are therefore of three possible types, those where the calculator is prohibited, those where it is necessary, and those where it makes no difference. For simplicity, this text identifies only those examples where the calculator is required and all other examples should be treated as possibly occurring in the non-calculator paper. You should therefore use your calculator **only** where you see the calculator icon displayed to the left of the question number.

You are encouraged to mark all your work yourself, referring to the answers at the back of the book, and to record your scores on the progress table provided. Ask your teacher about any questions which you cannot solve. Now get your thinking cap on, and good luck with the exam.

P.W.W & C.M.S.

COPYING PROHIBITED

Note: This publication is NOT licensed for copying under the Copyright Licensing Agency's Scheme, to which Robert Gibson & Sons are not party.

All rights reserved. No part of this publication may be reproduced; stored in a retrieval system; or transmitted in any form or by any means — electronic, mechanical, photocopying, or otherwise — without prior permission of the publisher Robert Gibson & Sons, Ltd., 17 Fitzroy Place, Glasgow, G3 7SF.

SET 1

1. Expand $(2x - 3y)(3x + 4y)$.
2. Factorise $3a^2 - ab - 2b^2$.
3. Express $\dfrac{3}{2\sqrt{5}}$ with a rational denominator.
4. Solve $(x - 2)^2 = 49$.
5. y varies as x^2 and $y = 4$ when $x = 4$. Find the formula relating x and y.
6. State the coordinates of the image of $(4, -3)$ under a half-turn about the point $(1, 4)$.
7. State the equation of the straight line passing through the point $(0, -3)$ with gradient 2.
8. Solve for x, $\cos x° = -0.873$, $180 \leq x \leq 360$.

SET 2

1. Simplify $(3x^2 - 2x + 5) - (x^2 + 6x - 9)$.
2. Express $\dfrac{3x}{2y} - \dfrac{2}{x}$ with a single denominator.
3. Simplify $\sqrt{a} \times \sqrt[3]{a}$.
4. Solve $\dfrac{x - 1}{2} < 5$.
5. Find the image of $(-5, 7)$ under
   (a) reflection in the y-axis;
   (b) half-turn about the origin.
6. P is $(-3, 4)$ and Q is $(7, -2)$. Write down the coordinates of the mid-point of PQ.
7. Write down the equation of the straight line passing through the points $(0, -3)$ and $(3, 0)$.
8. Calculate the length of BC.

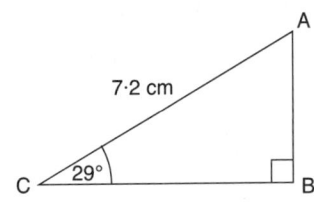

SET 3

1. Expand $(4x-3y)^2$.
2. Factorise $(a+1)^2 - b^2$.
3. Simplify $\sqrt{150} - \sqrt{54}$.
4. Solve $\frac{7}{8}y = \frac{5}{9}$.
5. Make b the subject of the formula $a = 2b - 5$.
6. Find the coordinates of the image of the point (4, 3) under a half-turn about (7, 2).
7. State the coordinates of the point where the line $3y = 2x + 4$ cuts the x-axis.
8. If $\tan\theta = \frac{8}{15}$ state the exact value of $\sin\theta$.

SET 4

1. Expand $(3x - y)(x - 2y)$.
2. If $f(x) = x^3 + 2x - 5$ evaluate $f(3)$.
3. Simplify $\frac{4a^4 \times 3a^3}{2a^{-2}}$.
4. State the coordinates of the minimum turning point of the parabola $y = (x-2)^2 + 5$.
5. "All prime numbers are odd". Provide a counter-example to prove that this statement is false.
6. Calculate the distance between A(6, 2) and B(8, 7) as a surd.
7. Find the equation of the line passing through (−6, 4) and the origin.
8. Express $\cos 237°$ in terms of the cosine of an acute angle.

SET 5

1. Evaluate $6 + 12 \div 3 - 4$.
2. $2\frac{5}{9} - 1\frac{3}{4}$.
3. If 8 oranges cost 20p what will 20 cost?
4. How long will a car take to travel 117 miles at 36 m.p.h.?
5. Convert $\frac{4}{9}$ to a percentage correct to 1 decimal place.
6. The average mark for class of 29 in a test is 32. If an absentee then sits the test and the average is now 31·6, find the mark scored by this pupil.
7. A firm promise to deliver within 70 days. When must an order be placed to ensure delivery by 5th December?.
8. A roomful of residents in a nursing home were comparing the number of great grandchildren they had and obtained this list of numbers:
    3   3   5   7   9   11   12   14   17   19   20.
    Find the semi-interquartile range of this data set.

SET 6

1. Factorise fully $8x^2 - 18y^2$.
2. Express $\frac{8}{\sqrt{12}}$ in its simplest form with a rational denominator.
3. Solve $2x^2 - 3x - 9 = 0$.
4. If x varies as the square of y and inversely as the square root of z state the formula connecting x, y and z if the constant of variation is $\frac{1}{2}$.
5. (a) Does the letter C have cyclic symmetry?
   (b) Does the letter Z have an axis of symmetry?
6. If the bearing of B from A is 075°, what is the bearing of A from B?
7. Calculate the length of the arc AB.
   [Use $\pi = 3\cdot 14$]

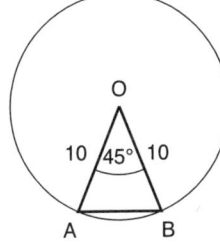

8. Calculate the length of QR.

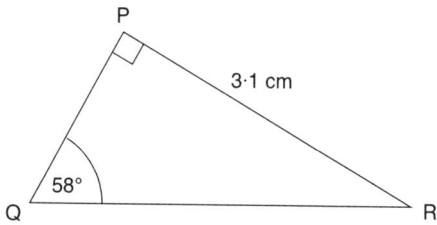

SET 7

1. If $a = -3$, $b = 2$, $c = -2$, evaluate $a^2 - c^2 - 2abc$.
2. Express $\dfrac{2}{a} - \dfrac{3}{2b}$ with a single denominator.
3. If $x = 16$, evaluate $3x^{-3/4}$.
4. What is the equation of the axis of symmetry of the parabola $f(x) = (x+2)(x-4)$?
5. Solve $3x + 2 < 11$.
6. ABCD, PQRS is a cube of side 1 m. Write down the length of a space diagonal in surd form.
7. Write down the gradient of the line $2x - 3y = 5$.
8. Write down the value of the cosine of the smallest angle of this triangle.

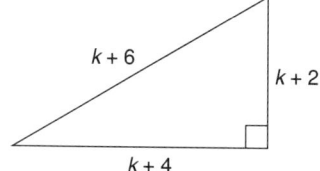

SET 8

1. Expand $(2x + 5y)(3x - 2y)$.
2. Simplify $\sqrt{128} - \sqrt{98}$.
3. Solve $2(x + 3) = 3(x - 4)$.
4. Make q the subject of the formula $y = 2p - 3q$.
5. A regular hexagon has 12 axes of symmetry. True or false?
6. If A is (8, 3) and B is (12, 9), write down the coordinates of the mid-point of AB.
7. Write down the equation of the straight line through (0, 5) and (5, 0).
8. Solve $\tan \theta° = -2 \cdot 097$ for $0 \leq \theta \leq 180$.

SET 9

1. Expand $(5x - 3y)^2$.
2. Simplify $\dfrac{a^2 \times a^3}{a^4}$.
3. What are the coordinates of the minimum turning point of the parabola $y = (x - 3)^2 - 7$?
4. Prove that for any integer n, $n(n + 1)$ is even.
5. Calculate x and y.

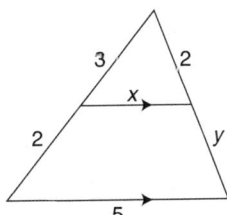

6. The foot of a 10 m ladder is 2 m from the foot of the wall against which it is leaning. Calculate, to 1 decimal place, how far up the wall the ladder reaches.
7. State the coordinates of the point where the line $y = 3 - 2x$ cuts the x-axis.
8. On a single diagram, sketch the graphs of $\sin x°$ and $\cos x°$ for $0 \leq x \leq 90$, labelling both clearly.

SET 10

1. Evaluate $9 - 3 \times 2 + 16 \div 4$.
2. Express 0·006 738 in standard form correct to 3 significant figures.
3. $2\frac{3}{7} \div 11\frac{1}{3}$.
4. The insurance rate on a property is £0.12 per £100. What premium must be paid on a £21 000 house?
5. If 27 men can do a job in 26 days, how many **more** men will be needed to do it in 18 days?
6. A man can buy a car either with £3500 cash or by putting down a deposit of £1000 followed by 24 monthly instalments of £125. How much more will be pay by the second method?
7. Calculate the percentage profit on articles bought for £5 per dozen and sold at 60p each.
8. A single card is drawn at random from a standard pack of cards. Write down the probability that the card drawn is:
   (a) red (b) a queen (c) a red queen.

SET 11

1. Simplify $4(a + 3c + 5d) - 3(2a - 5c + 4d)$.
2. Simplify $\sqrt{75} - \sqrt{27}$.
3. Solve $3(x + 8) = 2(x - 7)$.
4. If $y \propto x^2$, find p.
x	1	2	3
y	5	p	45
5. A film slide measures 30 mm across and 20 mm deep. If the projection of the slide on a screen is 42 cm across, how deep is it?
6. A is (3, 5) and B is (8, 9). Find the coordinates of the mid-point of AB.
7. Find the equation of the line passing through the origin and (6, 9).
8. Write down the value of the sine of the smallest angle of this triangle.

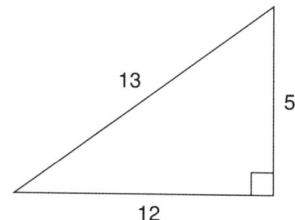

SET 12

1. Simplify $(3x^2 + y^2) - (2x^2 - 3y^2)$.
2. Factorise $(a+b)^2 - 4c^2$.
3. Simplify $a^{1/2} \div a^{3/2}$, expressing your answer with a positive index.
4. What are the coordinates of the maximum turning point on the graph of $y = 5 - (3-x)^2$?
5. Solve, $\left.\begin{array}{r}x - 2y = 0 \\ 3x + y = 14\end{array}\right\}$
6. If the bearing of A from B is 062°, what is the bearing of B from A?
7. PQ and RS are two diameters of the same circle. What shape must PSQR be?
8. Solve $\cos x° = \frac{1}{3}$ for $0 \le x \le 360$.

SET 13

1. Expand $(2x + 3y)^2$.
2. Simplify $\frac{a}{b} + \frac{b}{2a}$.
3. Express $\frac{3}{\sqrt{18}}$ in its simplest form with a rational denominator.
4. Make r the subject of the formula $h = 3 - 4r$.
5. OABC is a parallelogram with O(0, 0), A(4, 3), C(1, 5). Find the coordinates of B.
6. XPQR is a tetrahedron with XP, XQ and XR mutually perpendicular and of length 5, 12 and 9 units respectively. Which is longer, PQ or RQ, and by how much?

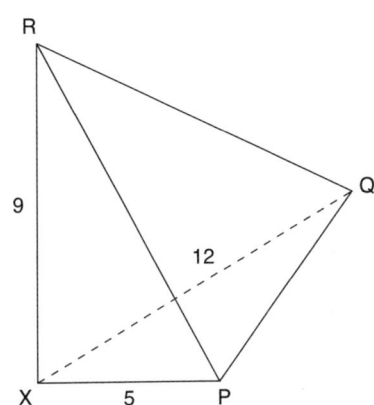

7. Write down the gradient of the line $x = 5y - 2$.

8. Calculate the size of $K\hat{L}M$.

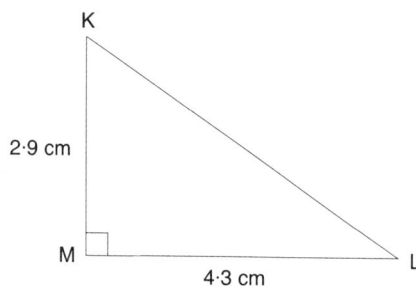

SET 14

1. Evaluate $2a^2b - 3bc^2$ when $a = -2$, $b = 3$ and $c = -5$.
2. Simplify $\dfrac{a^2 \times a^{-3}}{a^{-4}}$.
3. Write down the equation of the axis of symmetry of the parabola $y = (x - 1)(x - 5)$.
4. Find the image of $(3, -5)$ under
    (a) reflection in the x-axis (b) half-turn about the origin.
5. Write down the coordinates of the mid-point of AB where A is $(2, 1)$ and B is $(6, -3)$.
6. Write down the equation of the line passing through the origin parallel to $3x - y = 4$.
7. If $\cos \theta = \dfrac{24}{25}$, find the exact value of $\tan \theta$ if θ is acute.
8. Solve $\sin x° = 0$, $0 \leq x \leq 360$.

SET 15

1. Evaluate $37 - 15 + 55 \div 11$.
2. Evaluate $\sqrt{0\cdot000\,081}$.
3. What is the radius of a circle of area 154 cm² $\left(\text{take } \pi = \dfrac{22}{7}\right)$?
4. If 12 men take 154 hours to do a job how much **longer** would 7 men take?

5. How fast (in km / h) is a car going if it covers 33 km in 45 minutes?
6. Express $16\frac{2}{3}\%$ as a vulgar fraction in its lowest terms.
7. A batsman scores 31, 79, 0, 108 and 17 in his first five games. What must he score in his next game to average 50 runs per game?
8. Lay a ruler along what you consider to be the line of best fit on this scatter graph, find its equation and use it to estimate the value of y when $x = 2$.

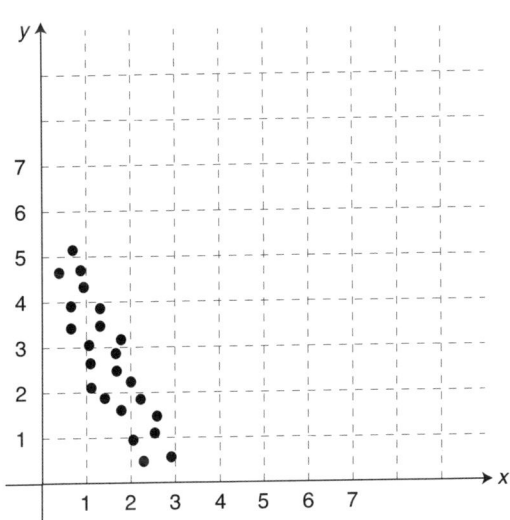

SET 16

1. If $f(x) = x^2 - 3x + 5$, evaluate $f(-3)$.
2. Expand $(2\sqrt{2} + 1)^2$.
3. Solve $\frac{2y}{3} = \frac{4}{5}$.
4. If $y \propto x^3$, find q. $\begin{array}{c|ccc} x & 1 & 2 & 3 \\ \hline y & 2 & q & 54 \end{array}$
5. Find the coordinates of R′, the image of R(5, 8) under a half-turn about the point (6, 4).
6. Calculate the length of a space diagonal of a cuboid measuring 8 cm × 6 cm × 5 cm. Express your answer as a surd in its simplest form.
7. Write down the equation of the line passing through (0, 0) and (−2, −4).
8. State the Sine Rule for triangle GHK.

SET 17

1. Factorise $5x^2 + 9xy - 2y^2$.
2. Write down the equation of the axis of symmetry of the parabola $y = (x+1)(x-7)$.
3. Solve $2x - 3 \geq 0$.
4. Find the area of a kite whose diagonals measure 3 cm and 8 cm.
5. Calculate the distance between A(–5, 7) and B(3, 1).
6. At what point does the line $x = 5y - 2$ cut the x-axis?
7. Solve $\sin x° + 1 = 0$ for $0 < x < 360$.
8. A 10 foot long ladder leans against a wall and makes an angle of 72° with level ground. Find the height of the top of the ladder above the ground.

SET 18.

1. Simplify $p^2 + q^2$ where $p = (a+b)$ and $q = (a-b)$.
2. Express as a single fraction $1 + \dfrac{x+1}{x}$.
3. Solve $(x+4)^2 = 25$.
4. Make t the subject of the formula $s = \dfrac{a}{t} - \dfrac{b}{t}$.
5. Two opposite angles of a kite are 40° and 60°. Find the size of each of the other angles.
6. State the bearing of A from B.

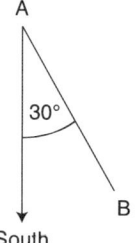

7. Write down the equation of the straight line passing through (0, –1) with gradient 2.

8. Find *x*.

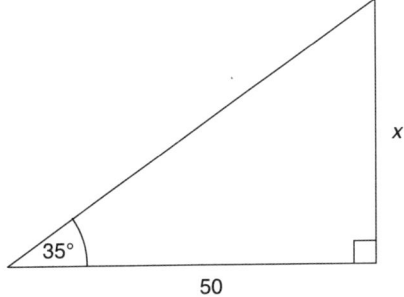

SET 19

1. Expand $(7x - y)^2$.
2. Factorise $(a - b)^2 - c^2$.
3. Write down the minimum value of the function $f(x) = (2x + 5)^2 + 1$.
4. Prove that the square of any odd integer has remainder 1 when divided by 4.
5. How long is the diagonal of a 5 cm square? Express your answer as a surd in its simplest form.
6. O is the centre of the circle.
   $A\hat{C}O = 40°$, $O\hat{B}A = 25°$.
   Calculate the size of $B\hat{O}C$.

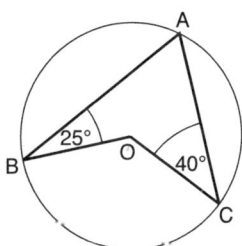

 7. Solve $\tan x° = -1\cdot 3$, $0 \leq x \leq 180$.

8. Write down the maximum value of
   (a) $\sin 2x°$ (b) $2 \sin x°$.

SET 20

1. Express $(3\cdot 2 \times 10^5) \times (2\cdot 6 \times 10^2)$ in standard form correct to 2 significant figures.
2. $4\frac{1}{9} \div 6\frac{1}{6}$.

3. A house is valued at £18 500. If the cost of insurance is 15p per £100, calculate the annual premium.
4. 10 bags of sugar weigh 25 lbs. How many bags weigh 10 lbs?
5. What is the average speed of a homing pigeon which covers 132 km in $2\frac{3}{4}$ hours?
6. A cycle cost £65. I put down 10% deposit and pay the rest in 9 instalments. What is the amount of each instalment?
7. A dozen articles cost £40. They are sold at £3.50 each. Find the percentage profit.
8. A group of S4 pupils counted how many books each had in their schoolbag and the following frequency table was obtained.

Number of books	7	8	9	10	11	12
Frequency	12	14	15	19	17	3

If one of these pupils is chosen at random, what is the probability of that pupil having more than ten books in his / her schoolbag?

SET 21

1. Expand $(2x + 3y)(3x - 2y)$.
2. Find $f(2)$ if $f(x) = 2^{x+1}$.
3. Express $\frac{1}{\sqrt{50}}$ in its simplest form with a rational denominator.
4. Solve $x^2 - 5x + 6 = 0$.
5. If $y \propto \sqrt[3]{x}$ and $y = 4$ when $x = 8$, write down the equation connecting x and y.
6. Find x.

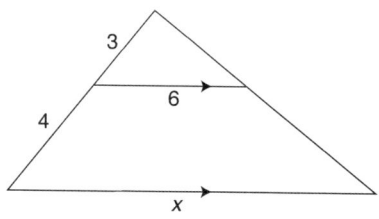

7. What is the gradient of the line $3x + 4y = 12$?
8. Calculate the length of PR.

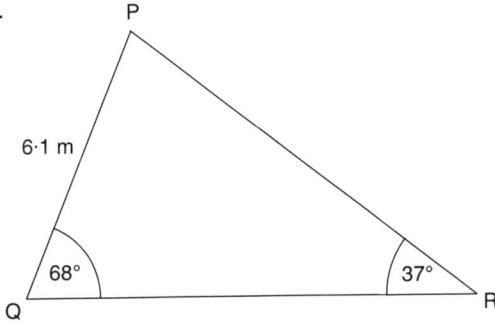

SET 22

1. If $a = 4$, $b = -2$, $c = -1$, evaluate $2ab^2 + 3bc^3$.
2. Evaluate $(25)^{3/2}$.
3. Make q the subject of the formula $p + \frac{1}{3}q = r$.
4. The edges of two cubes are in the ratio 2:3. Write down the ratio of their volumes.
5. How long is the diagonal of a square of side t units?
6. Give the coordinates of the point where the line $3x + 4y = 12$ cuts the x-axis.
7. Calculate the value of $\tan G\hat{A}F$ given $AB = 6$, $BF = 8$, $FG = 7$.

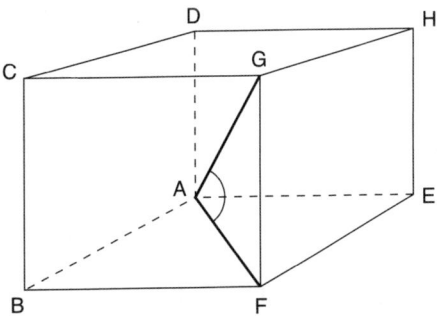

8. State the Cosine Rule for p^2 in triangle PQR.

SET 23

1. Simplify $7a^3 + 4b^2 - (2a^3 - 3b^2)$.
2. Factorise $6x^2 + 25x - 9$.
3. Simplify $\sqrt{98} - \sqrt{32}$.
4. Solve $x^2 + x - 2 = 0$.
5. Solve $5 - 3x > 0$.
6. Calculate the distance between A(2, −1) and B(−4, −9).
7. State the equation of OP when P is (−3, 1).

8. Find x if $\sin x° = 2 \sin 25°$ and $x < 90$.

SET 24

1. Expand $(3x + y)^2$.
2. Simplify $\dfrac{x^2 - 2x + 1}{x^2 - x}$.
3. Evaluate $64^{2/3} + 16^{-1/4}$.
4. Write down the coordinates of the turning point of the graph of $y = (x + 2)^2 - 6$.
5. Prove that for any integer n, 6 is a factor of $n^3 - n$.
6. Solve $1 + \cos x° = 0$ for $0 < x < 360$.
7. What is the length of arc AB?
$\left[\text{Use } \pi = \dfrac{22}{7} \right]$

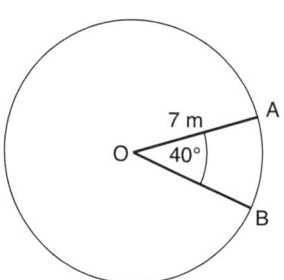

8. Write down the equation of the line through the point (3, −2) which
   (a) is parallel to the x-axis,
   (b) is parallel to the y-axis,
   (c) passes through the origin.

SET 25

1. Evaluate $5 + 3 \div \frac{1}{2}$.
2. Evaluate $\sqrt{11\frac{1}{9}}$ exactly.
3. 11 men decide to hire a mini bus at a cost of £1.98 each to take them to a football match. If only 9 men can manage to go, how much would they pay each?
4. What is the total surface area of a cuboid measuring 3 cm × 4 cm × 5 cm?
5. A car takes 2 hours 20 minutes to travel 98 miles. Calculate the average speed.
6. A man earns £88 per week. He gets an increase of 18%. Calculate his new wage.
7. After 8 innings a batsman averages 50 runs per innings. In his next innings he scores 131. What is his average now?
8. A primary school class were comparing shoe sizes and obtained the following frequency table.

Shoe size	7	8	9	10	11	12
Frequency	3	5	7	8	4	3

   Calculate the semi-interquartile range of this frequency distribution.

SET 26

1. Expand $(2x - y)^2$.
2. Factorise $6x^2 - 5x + 1$.
3. Express $\frac{3}{\sqrt{7}}$ with a rational denominator.
4. Solve $\begin{cases} 2x + y = 7 \\ y = x - 5 \end{cases}$.
5. Express as an equation "y varies as the square root of x and inversely as z".
6. Write down the gradient of the line $2x - 3y = 5$.

7. $\sin \alpha = \frac{12}{13}$, $\alpha < 90°$. Write down the exact value of $\tan \alpha$.

8. Write down an expression for the length of PQ.

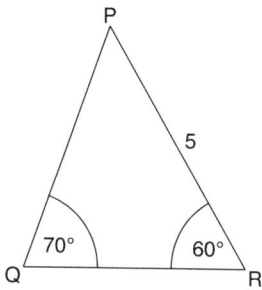

SET 27

1. A rectangle is $(2x + 7)$ units long and $(x - 3)$ units broad. Write down an expression in its simplest form for the perimeter.
2. If $g(x) = 3^{7-x}$, evaluate $g(4)$.
3. State whether the graph of the function $3x^2 - 2x + 4$ has a maximum or minimum turning point.
4. Write down the coordinates of the point of intersection of the lines whose equations are $x = 2$ and $2x + y = 1$.
5. State the coordinates of the mid-point of AB where A is $(-1, 5)$ and B$(-3, -3)$.
6. Where does the line $3x - 4y + 12 = 0$ cut the y-axis?
7. Solve $\sin x° = \frac{1}{4}$, $0 < x < 180$.
8. State the Cosine Rule for $\cos \hat{S}$ in $\triangle$RST.

SET 28

1. Evaluate $75^2 - 25^2$ by factorising.
2. Simplify $\sqrt{72} - \sqrt{50}$.
3. Solve $x^2 + 1 = 10$.
4. Make h the subject of the formula $V = \frac{1}{3}\pi r^2 h$.

5. Find the area of a kite whose diagonals measure 7 cm and 5 cm.
6. Fin the length of the space diagonal PY.

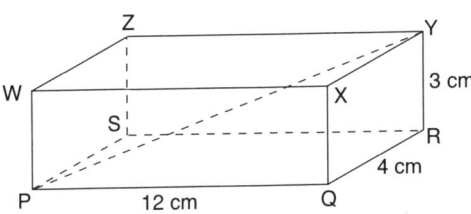

7. Write down the gradient of the line $3x + 2y = 7$.
8. In triangle ABC, $a = 9$ cm, $c = 6$ cm, $\hat{B} = 30°$. Calculate the area of the triangle.

SET 29

1. Simplify $\dfrac{5p}{2q} - \dfrac{2}{p}$.

2. Simplify $\dfrac{a^{2/3} \times a^{3/4}}{(a^{2/3})^{3/4}}$.

3. Write down the equation of the axis of symmetry of the graph of $y = (x-2)(x-7)$.

4. "In any triangle ABC, the median from A and the altitude from A meet BC in separate points." Provide a counter-example to show that this statement is not always true.

5. The angles of a triangle are in the ratio 2:3:5. Find the size of the largest angle.

6. C(2, 5) is the mid-point of AB. If A is (1, 2), give the coordinates of B.

7. The lines $2x - 3y + 5 = 0$, $y = -3$ and $x = k$ are concurrent. Find the value of k.

8. Express sin 292° in terms of the sine of an acute angle.

SET 30

1. Evaluate $12(15 - 9) \div 3 + 1$.
2. Express $(1\cdot05 \times 10^3) \times (4\cdot0 \times 10^4)$ in standard form correct to 1 significant figure.
3. 2 pumps empty a tank in half an hour. How long would 3 pumps have taken?
4. If the rate of exchange is 2·47 Swiss francs to the £, how many francs would you get for £85?
5. A boy bought 12 marbles at the rate of 4 marbles for 3p from one friend and sold them to another friend at the rate of 3 marbles for 4p. What was his actual profit?
6. A certain car mechanic is paid £6 per hour. What does he earn for an 8-hour shift followed by 2 hours overtime at time and a half?
7. A farmer sells potatoes in 25 kg bags for £2.20 each. What is his crop of 50 000 kg worth to him?
8. Make an array of all the possible outcomes of throwing two dice and hence calculate the probability of the total score exceeding 7.

SET 31

1. Factorise $6a^2 - ab - b^2$.
2. Express with a rational denominator in its simplest terms $\dfrac{6}{5\sqrt{2}}$.
3. Solve $(x + 2)^2 = 1$.
4. x varies as the square root of y and inversely as the cube of z. Express this as an equation.
5. The bearing of A from B is 212°. State the bearing of B from A.
6. What is the length of the radius of this circle?

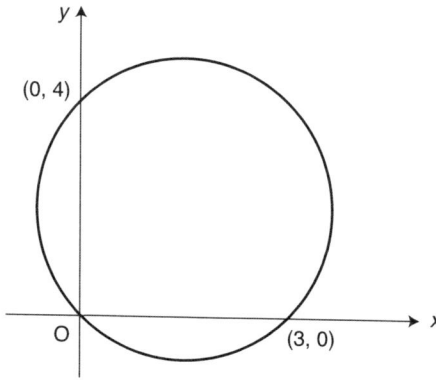

7. $\cos x° = -\cos 56°$. Find x if $0 < x < 360$.
8. The area of $\triangle PQR$ is 20 cm². $PQ = 5$ cm and $QR = 10$ cm. If $P\hat{Q}R$ is acute, find its size.

SET 32

1. Expand $(3xy - 7z)^2$.
2. Evaluate $f(1)$ when $f(x) = (x + 2)^2 - 6$.
3. Evaluate $(2^0 + 2^4 + 2^6)^{1/2}$.
4. Write down the maximum value of $6 - (x - 1)^2$.
5. Calculate the lengths of OP and OQ.

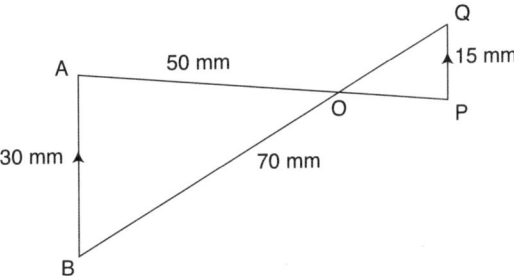

6. If P is (3, 1) and Q (−1, 5) find, as a surd, the distance PQ.
7. Solve $2 + \tan x° = 0$ for $0 < x < 360$.
8. Evaluate $a^2 + b^2 - 2ab \cos \hat{C}$ when $a = 8$, $b = 6$ and $C = 75.5°$.

SET 33

1. Factorise fully $\pi x^2 - \pi y^2$.
2. Express $\dfrac{3\sqrt{2}}{4\sqrt{5}}$ with a rational denominator.
3. Solve $3x^2 + 5x - 3 = 0$, expressing the roots correct to one decimal place.
4. Make k the subject of the formula $p = 2(k - q)$.

5. Find x.

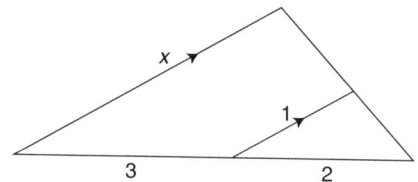

6. A is (–4, 1) and B(2, 9).
   (a) Write down the coordinates of the mid-point of AB.
   (b) Calculate the length of AB.

7. What is the equation of a line with gradient $\frac{-2}{3}$ which cuts the y-axis at $\left(0, \frac{2}{3}\right)$.

8. If $\cos \theta° = \frac{8}{17}$, find the exact value of $\sin \theta°$ when $\theta < 90$.

SET 34

1. Expand $(3a + b)(2a - 3b)$.
2. Factorise $12x^2 - x - 6$.
3. Solve $x^{3/2} = 8$.
4. Write down the equation of the axis of symmetry of the graph of $f: x \to (x+4)^2 - 6$.
5. Prove that for $0 < x < 90$, $\sin(90 - \theta)° = \cos \theta°$.
6. Where does the line $y = 5 - 4x$ cut the x-axis?
7. Solve $\tan x° = -1·505$ for $0 < x < 360$.
8. Write down the maximum value of $(1 + 5\sin\theta)^2$.

SET 35

These ten questions refer to the line $3x - 2y = 6$.

1. State the coordinates of the point A on the x-axis.
2. State the coordinates of the point B on the y-axis.
3. Calculate the area of $\triangle AOB$.

4. State the gradient of AB.

5. Calculate (as a surd) the length of AB.

6. Using your answers to questions 3 and 5, calculate the length of the altitude of △AOB from O, expressing your answer with a rational denominator.

7. State the equation of the line through the origin parallel to the given line.

8. Find the equation of the given line after it has been translated 2 units up the y-axis.

SET 36

1. Simplify $(a - b) - (b - c) - (c - a)$.

2. Express $1 + \dfrac{1}{x}$ as a single fraction.

3. Simplify $\dfrac{\sqrt{50} - \sqrt{18}}{\sqrt{98}}$.

4. Solve $6x^2 - x - 1 = 0$.

5. Where does the line $2y = x - 1$ cut the y-axis?

6. Express south-west as a three figure bearing.

7. In deciding how much to pay out on claims for thefts of videos, an insurance company reckons that they depreciate each year by 10% of their value at the start of that year. If one client paid £400 for her video two years ago, how much can she expect to be reimbursed if it is stolen?

8. Calculate the standard deviation of the following scores:

9   11   12   16   18   19   21   23   24

using the formula $\sigma = \sqrt{\dfrac{\Sigma(x - \bar{x})^2}{n}}$.

23

SET 37

1. Factorise $x^2y^2 - 9$.
2. If $x = 9$, evaluate $2x^{-1/2}$.
3. State the coordinates of the point where the parabola $y = 3x^2 - 2x + 4$ cuts the y-axis.
4. Solve $3 - x < 2x$.
5. Find the coordinates of the image of F(6, 5) under half-turn about G(4, 2).
6. AB is a chord 4 cm long of the circle centre O, OC = $\sqrt{3}$ cm. Calculate the area of the circle. $\left[\text{Use } \pi = \frac{22}{7} \right]$

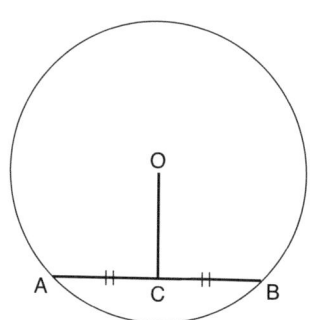

7. ABCD, EFGH is a cube of side 2 units. Write down the tangent of $H\hat{B}D$.

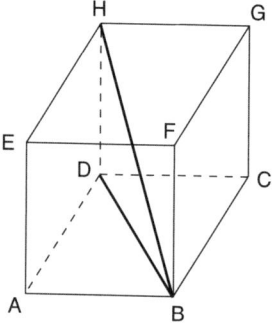

8. Write down the formula for $\cos \hat{P}$ in triangle PQR.

SET 38.

1. Find $f(2)$ if $f(x) = 3x^2 - 2x + 4$.
2. Simplify $\dfrac{\sqrt{18} - \sqrt{8}}{\sqrt{18}}$.
3. State the formula for solving $ax^2 + bx + c = 0$.
4. Change the subject of $A = 4\pi r^2$ to r.
5. Find the coordinates of the image of $A(-4, 3)$ under a clockwise quarter-turn about the origin.
6. Give the bearing of P from Q as a three figure bearing.

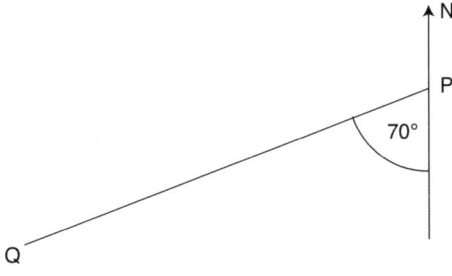

7. What is the gradient of the line $2y = x - 1$?
8. Write down the value of $\tan \theta$.

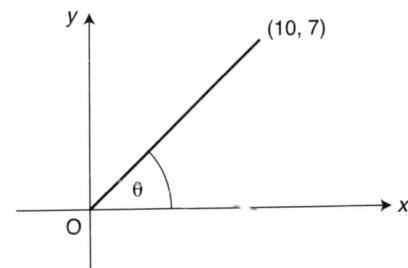

SET 39

1. Expand $(2a - b)(3a + 2b)$.
2. Factorise $2x^2 - 3x + 1$.
3. Evaluate 3^{-n} when $n = 4$.
4. "Every line in the x, y plane has an equation of the form $y = mx + c$." Provide a counter-example to show that this statement is false.
5. A is (3, 2), B(8, 2) and C(5, 0). Calculate the area of the quadrilateral OABC.

6. Give the gradient of PQ where P is (−2, −1) and Q(6, −3).
7. Find the equation of the line through (−2, 0) and (0, 4).
8. Sketch the sine graph for $0 \leq x \leq 360$.

SET 40

For these questions, P is the point (−2, 3) and Q(1, −1).
1. Calculate the length of PQ.
2. Write down the coordinates of M, the mid-point of PQ.
3. Write down the equation of OM.
4. Find the gradient of PQ.
5. Find the coordinates of the image of P under a half-turn about Q.
6. Write down the image of P under reflection in the line $y = x$.
7. Write down the image of Q under reflection in the line $x + y = 0$.
8. Write down the size of the angle between OQ and the x-axis.

SET 41

1. Simplify $2(6x - y) - 3(y - 3x) - 5x$.
2. Simplify $\dfrac{x^2 - 1}{x^2 - x - 2}$.
3. Express $\dfrac{2}{3\sqrt{5}}$ with a rational denominator.
4. Solve $x^2 + 3x - 4 = 0$.
5. $y = \dfrac{k}{x^2}$ where k is a constant. When $x = 3$, $y = 4$. Find y when $x = 6$.
6. Write down the equation of the straight line through the origin parallel to $3y + 2x = 5$.
7. Given that $\tan x = \dfrac{4}{3}$ and x is acute, write down the exact value of sin x.

8. Calculate the value of x.

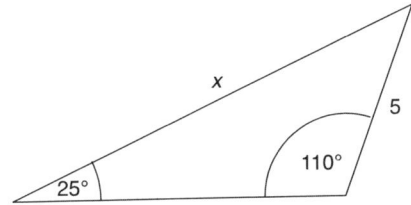

SET 42

1. A man borrows £1000 on 1st February 1990 and is charged 10% interest every 1st February thereafter on the amount he was still due to repay on the previous 1st February. He repays £500 on 31st January 1991 and 31st January 1992. How much does he still owe?
2. Factorise fully $3x^2 - 27y^2$.
3. What is the equation of the axis of symmetry of the graph of $y = x^2 + 4x - 5$?
4. Write down the point of intersection of the lines $x = 3$ and $y = 3 - 3x$.
5. Calculate the area of a 3, 4, 5 triangle.
6. Write down the equations of the lines through A(5, 3) parallel to Ox and Oy.
7. Solve $\cos x° = -0.334$, $0 \le x \le 360$.
8. Find the value of $\cos Y\hat{X}Z$.

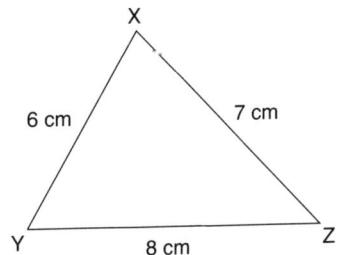

SET 43

1. Simplify $(x - 3y)^2 - (2y - x)(y - 2x)$.
2. Find the image of (-4) under the function $f: x \to 5 - 2x - x^2$.
3. Simplify $\sqrt{8} + \sqrt{32}$.

4. $y = ax + b$. Change the subject to x.
5. Find x and y.

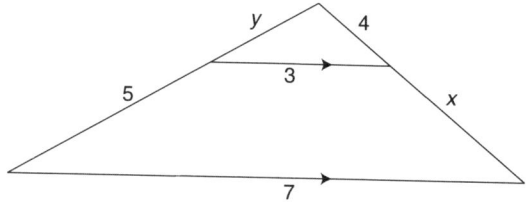

6. Express 25° west of north as a three figure bearing.
7. PQ is a diameter and O the centre of the circle. $P\hat{Q}R = 56$. Find the size of $P\hat{R}O$.

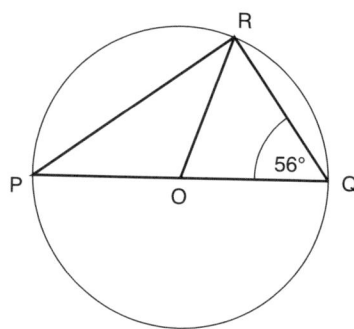

8. Find the value of $2\cos^2 x° + 3$ when $x = 180$.

SET 44

1. Evaluate $12{\cdot}5^2 - 7{\cdot}5^2$ by factorising.
2. Simplify $\dfrac{(ab)^{-2}}{a^{-2}b^3}$.
3. $y = (6-x)(2+x)$. What is the turning point of the graph of this function?
4. "Every quadratic equation has two different solutions." Provide a counter-example to show that this statement is false.
5. Two circles have radii of 6 cm and 9 cm. What is the ratio of their areas?
6. Find the equation of the line through (1, 0) and (0, 5).

7. Write down the value of the cosine of the smallest angle of this triangle.

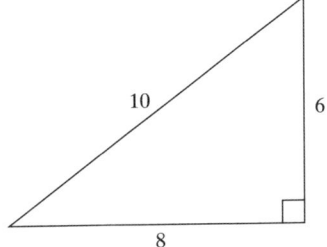

8. Write down the value of tan θ.

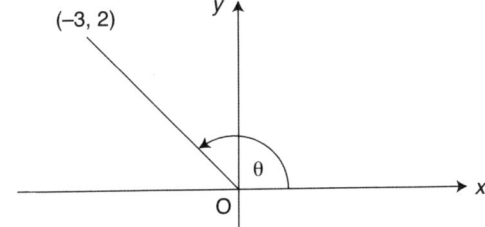

SET 45

For Questions 1–4 use this diagram, where O is the centre of the circle.

∠ROT = 150°, PR and PT are tangents.

1. What size is ∠TPR?
2. Find the area of sector TOR.
3. Find the area of △TOR.
4. Find the length of PT.

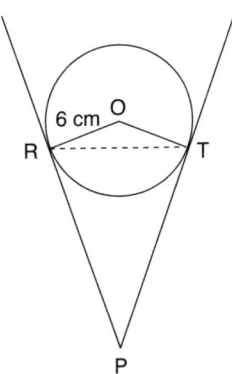

In Questions 5–8, $f(x) = x^2 - 2x - 15$

5. Find the roots of $f(x) = 0$.
6. Write down the equation of the axis of symmetry of the graph of $f(x)$.
7. Find the minimum value of $f(x)$.
8. Write down the coordinates of the point where the graph of $f(x)$ crosses the y-axis.

SET 46

1. A cuboid measures $2x$ m by $3x$ m by $5x$ m. Find its total surface area in square metres (in terms of x).

2. Solve $5x^2 + 2x - 1 = 0$ correct to 3 decimal places.
3. If x varies directly as y and inversely as z, by what is x multiplied when y is doubled and z is halved?
4. Find the coordinates of the image of B(−5, −4) under reflection in the line $y = 4$.
5. P is (3, 1) and Q(−1, 5). Find the gradient of PQ.
6. Write down the equation of the line through (0, 5) parallel to $2x - y = 0$.

7. Solve $\cos x° = -0.542$ for $0 \leq x \leq 360$.
8. Lay a ruler along what you consider to be the line of best fit on this scatter graph, find its equation and use it to estimate the value of y when $x = 2$.

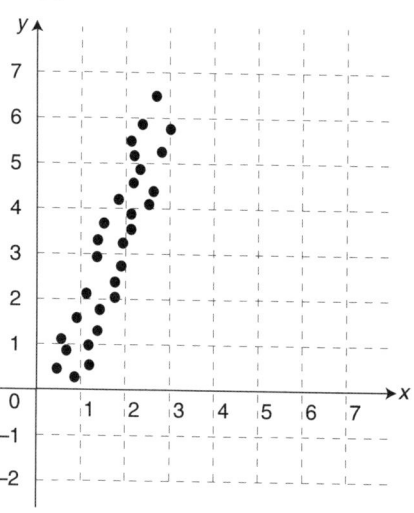

SET 47

1. Is it better to invest £100 at 9% interest per annum compounded half-yearly or at 8% per annum compounded quarterly? [And by how much in the first year?]

2. Express $2 + \dfrac{x}{y}$ as a single fraction.
3. Evaluate $64^{-2/3}$ by applying the laws of indices.
4. Sketch the graph of $y = x^2 - 4$.
5. Solve $2(3x - 2) \leq 2$.
6. Write down the coordinates of the image of point $(4, -3)$ when it is given a half-turn about the point $(1, 1)$.
7. Find the mid-point of AB if A is $(6, -3)$ and $B(-2, -1)$.
8. The line $x + 2y = 6$ cuts the coordinate axes at P and Q. Calculate the area of triangle POQ.

SET 48

1. Expand $(2x - 3y)(5x + 4y)$.
2. Factorise $6x^2 - 5x - 6$.
3. The length of the side of a square is $2\sqrt{3}$ cm. Find its area in cm^2.
4. Solve $2(5x - 1) = 3 - 2(2 - x)$.
5. $I = \dfrac{Prn}{100}$. Change the subject to r.
6. Find k if $(2, k)$ lies on the line $3x + 2y = 12$.
7. ABCD, EFGH is a cuboid with AB = 4, AD = 4 and BF = 6. M is the mid-point of CG. Write down the tangent of $D\hat{M}A$.

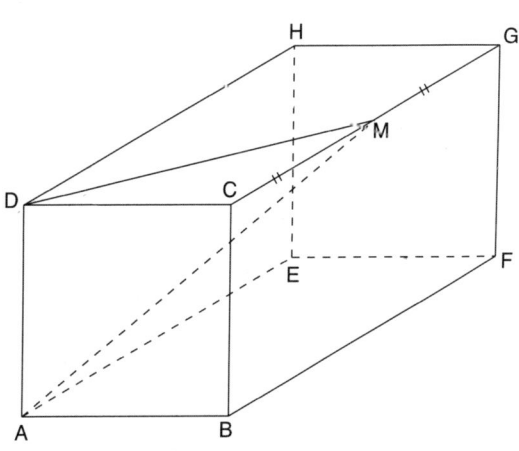

 8. ABCD is a rhombus with AB = 5 cm and $B\hat{A}D = 40°$. Find its area.

SET 49

1. Evaluate $m^0 - p^{-2}$ when $p = 8$ and $m = 25$.
2. Write down the coordinates of the turning point of the graph of $f(x) = 5 - (x - 2)^2$.
3. Prove that the square of every even number is divisible by 4.
4. State the image of $(3, -5)$ under reflection in $y = x$.
5. Show in a sketch the bearing 210°.
6. AC and BC are equal chords of a circle, centre O. The tangents to the circle at A and B meet at T. $\hat{BCO} = 50°$. Calculate the size of $\hat{ATB}$.

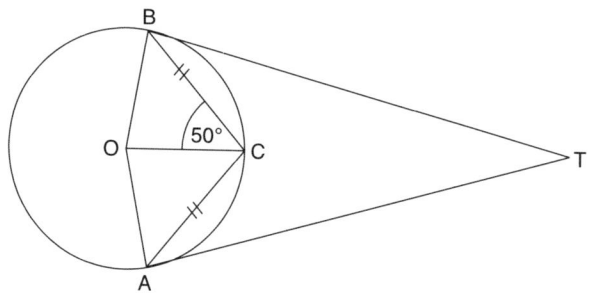

7. Write down the value of tan $\hat{XOA}$.

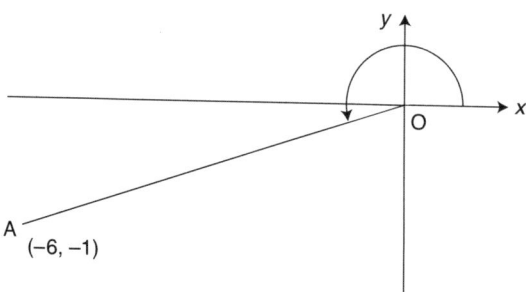

8. Sketch the cosine curve for $0 \le x \le 360$.

SET 50

Which graph, A, B, C, D, E, F, G, H, I or J has equation:

1. $y = x^2$
2. $y = x^2 + 1$
3. $y = x^2 - 1$
4. $y = (x - 1)^2$
5. $y = (x + 1)^2$
6. $y = -x^2$
7. $y = 1 - x^2$
8. $y = -1 - x^2$
9. $y = -(x - 1)^2$
10. $y = -(x + 1)^2$

A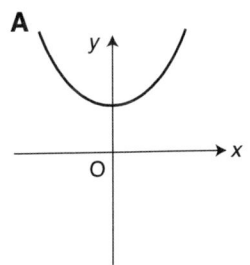

B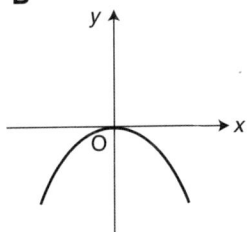

C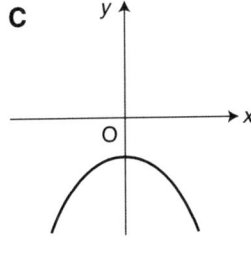

D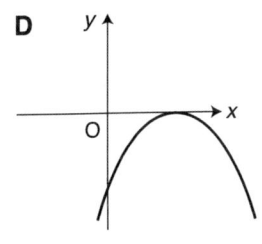

E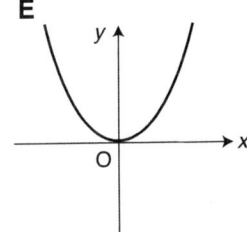

F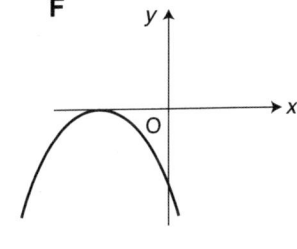

G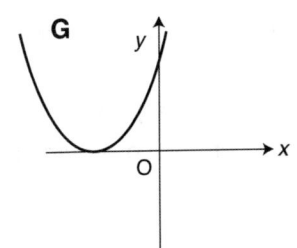

H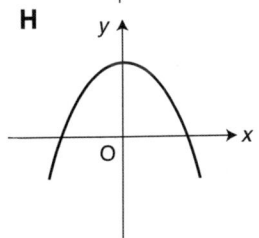

I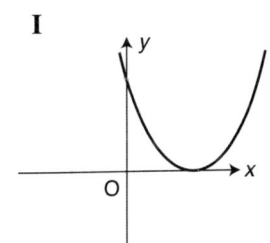

J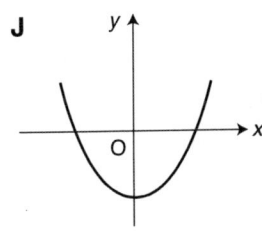

SET 51
1. Expand $(3x - y)(2y + x)$.
2. Factorise $x^4 - 16$.
3. Simplify $\sqrt{20} + \sqrt{80}$.
4. Solve $3(2x - 5) - 2(3 - x) = 0$.
5. If y varies as the square of x and inversely as the square root of z, what effect on y will doubling x and quartering z have?
6. Calculate the area of a rhombus whose diagonals measure 6 cm and 8 cm.
7. Find the equation of the line through $(-3, 0)$ and $(0, 9)$.
8. Sketch the graph of $y = \cos 2x°$ for $0 < x < 360$.

SET 52
1. Simplify $\dfrac{x^2 + x - 6}{2x^2 - 18}$.
2. Simplify $\dfrac{p^{-4} \times p^6}{(p^{-4})^{1/2}}$.
3. Sketch the graph of $y = 9 - x^2$.
4. Solve $6 - 2x > x$.
5. How many axes of symmetry has
   (a) a parallelogram,   (b) a square?
6. OPQR is a rhombus with O(0, 0), P(4, 3) and R(3, 4). Find the coordinates of Q.
7. Find the equation of the line through $(0, -1)$ parallel to $5y = x - 3$.
8. Calculate the length of a chord of a circle of radius 3 cm which subtends an angle of 70° at the centre.

SET 53
1. Find the value of pq when $p = 2 \times 10^3$ and $q = 5 \times 10^{-3}$.
2. Factorise fully $3x^2 - 6x + 3$.
3. Simplify $\sqrt{18} - \sqrt{32} + \sqrt{50}$.
4. Solve $x^2 + x - 6 = 0$.

5. In how many ways does (a) a kite, (b) a rectangle fit its own outline?
6. (a) Calculate the volume of a cuboid measuring 9 cm by 8 cm by 3 cm.
   (b) What would be the edge length of a cube with the same volume?
7. Solve $\cos x° = -\sin 20°$ for $0 \leq x \leq 360$.
8. Express $\dfrac{\triangle AOB}{\triangle BOC}$ in terms of x and y.

   [$\triangle AOB$ denotes the area of triangle AOB.]

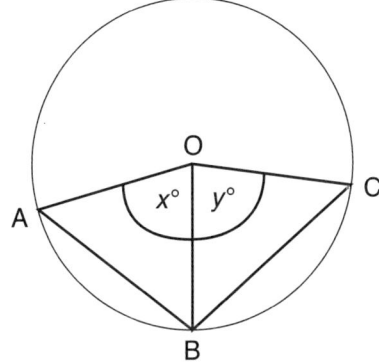

SET 54

1. Expand $(a - b)(a + 2b - c)$.
2. If $f(x) = \dfrac{3x^2 - 1}{x}$, find the value of $f(-2)$.
3. Evaluate $(27)^{-4/3}$.
4. Sketch $y = x^2$ and $y = 2x^2$ on the same diagram.
5. A scale model of a bus is 8 cm long and 3 cm wide. If the actual length of the bus is 6 m, what is its width?
6. P is the point $(a + b, a - b)$ and Q is $(a - b, b - a)$. Find the coordinates of the mid-point of PQ.
7. Find r if $(r, -3)$ lies on the line $3x - 4y = 9$.
8. Simplify $\cos(90 - a)° - \sin(360 - a)°$.

SET 55

Which graph, A, B, C or D, has equation:

1. $y = \dfrac{12}{x}$ **2.** $y = \dfrac{-12}{x}$ **3.** $y = 12^x$ **4.** $y = 12^{-x}$

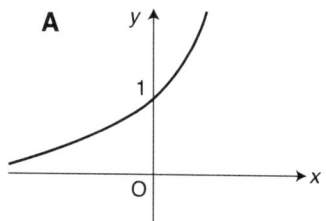

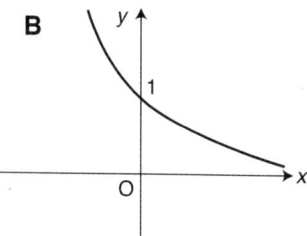

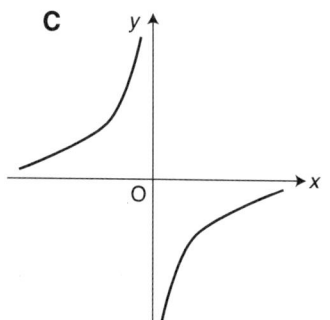

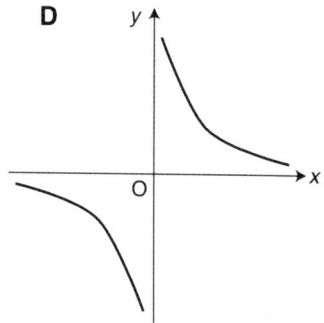

Questions 5 to 8 refer to the following frequency table.

Age	17	18	19	20	21	22
Frequency	1	2	5	8	6	3

The ages of 25 people in a bus going to a disco were noted and the above frequency table obtained.

5. Write down (i) the mode and (ii) the range.
6. Find (i) the median and (ii) the semi-interquartile range.
7. Calculate the mean age of the people on the bus.
8. Write down the value of $x - \bar{x}$ for each of the 25 ages and hence calculate the standard deviation using the formula $\sigma = \sqrt{\dfrac{\Sigma(x-\bar{x})^2}{n}}$

SET 56
1. $A = (2x + y)$ and $B = (y - 3x)$. Express $A^2 - AB$ in terms of x and y.
2. Factorise fully $x^3 - 4x$.
3. Express $\dfrac{2}{\sqrt{18}}$ with rational denominator in its simplest form.
4. Calculate the length of AC.

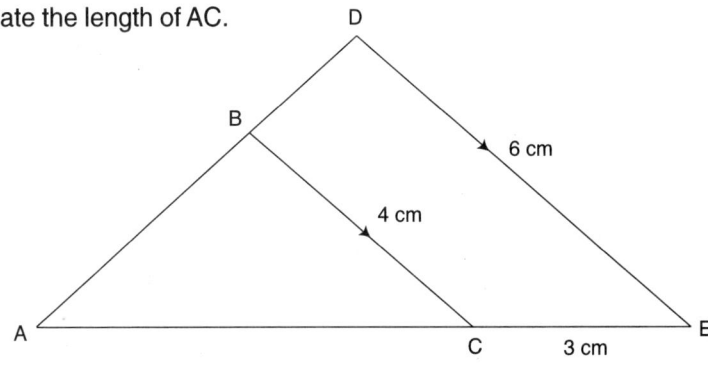

5. In this farm gate $A\hat{C}F = 60°$. What size is $B\hat{G}F$?

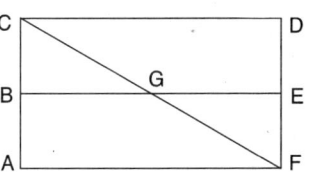

6. In a circle with centre O and radius 18 cm, $A\hat{O}B = 75°$. Calculate the length of arc AB.
7. A vertical pole 7 m high casts a shadow 10 m long on level ground. Calculate the angle of elevation of the sun.
8. In $\triangle WXY$, $WX = 7\cdot86$, $W\hat{X}Y = 47\cdot1°$ and $W\hat{Y}X = 39\cdot5°$. Find the length of WY.

SET 57
1. Expand $(5x - 3y)(2x + 7y)$.
2. Factorise $3\cos^2 x° - 2\cos x° - 1$.
3. Evaluate $16^{-3/4}$.
4. Sketch the graph of $y = (x - 1)^2$ on plain paper.
5. Solve $\left.\begin{array}{l} x + y = 9 \\ x - y = 7 \end{array}\right\}$

6. This is the net of a square pyramid. AC is 10 units long. What is the height of the pyramid when it is built up?

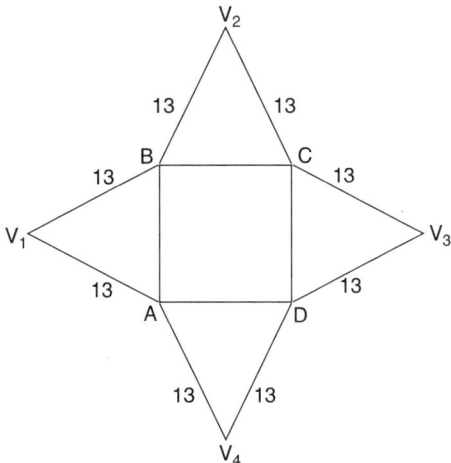

7. Find the equation of the straight line through (2, 0) and (0, 1).

8. Calculate the size of $A\hat{O}B$.

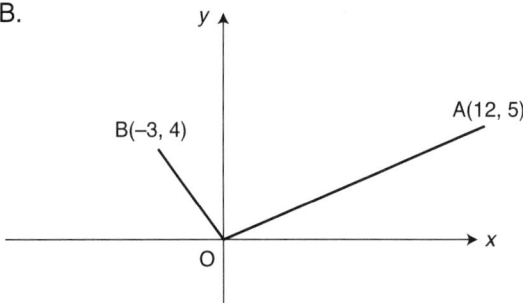

SET 58

1. Expand and simplify $x(y-z) - y(z-x) - z(x-y)$.

2. Express $\dfrac{3p}{4q} - \dfrac{4q}{3p}$ as a single fraction.

3. Simplify $\sqrt{8} + \dfrac{4}{\sqrt{2}}$.

4. Solve $\dfrac{2}{3}x = \dfrac{7}{5}$.

5. Make c the subject of the formula $W = \dfrac{b-c}{c}$.

6. Find the image of (2, −4) under a half-turn about (−1, 3).
7. ABCD is a kite. Calculate its area.

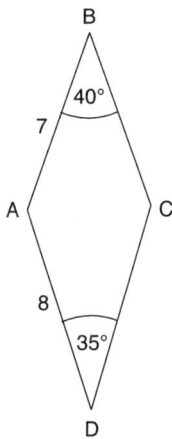

8. Two spinners are numbered 1 to 5. Make an array of all the possible outcomes of spinning both and hence calculate the probability of the scores on the two spinners being equal.

SET 59
1. Factorise $5x^2 - 20y^4$ fully.
2. If $2^{3x} = \frac{1}{8}$, find x.
3. On one diagram, sketch the graphs of $y = x^2$ and $y = -x^2$.
4. "For any integer n, $n^2 + n + 5$ is a prime number." Provide a counter-example to disprove this statement.
5. P is $(a, b-3)$ and Q is $(a+4, b)$. Calculate the length of AB.
6. Find k if the lines $2x + 3y = k$, $x = 3$ and $y = 4$ are concurrent.
7. If $\tan x° = \frac{4}{3}$ and $x < 90$, find the exact value of $\cos x°$.
8. Draw the graph of $y = \cos x° + 1$ for $0 \leq x \leq 360$.

SET 60

Which graph A, B, C, D, E, F, G or H has equation
1. $y = \sin 2x$
2. $y = \cos 2x$
3. $y = 2 \sin x$
4. $y = 2 \cos x$
5. $y = \sin \frac{1}{2}x$
6. $y = \cos \frac{1}{2}x$
7. $y = -\sin 2x$
8. $y = 2 \cos \frac{1}{2}x$

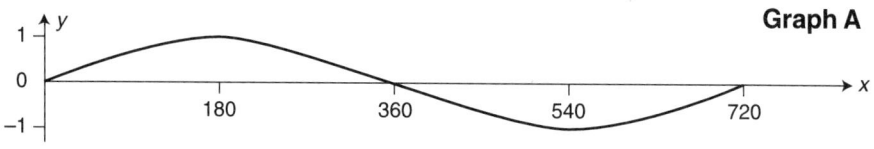

Graph A

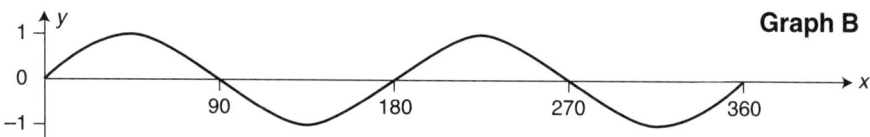

Graph B

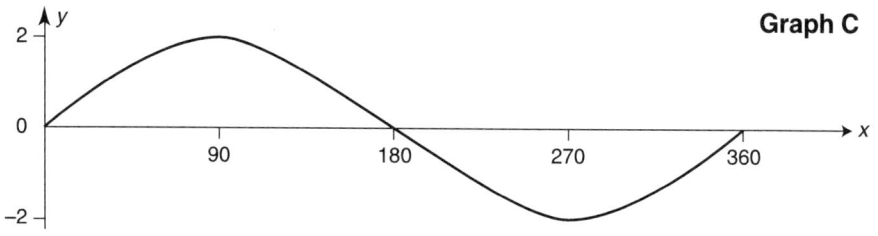

Graph C

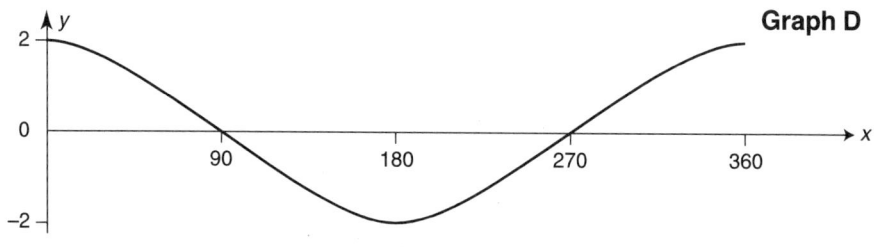

Graph D

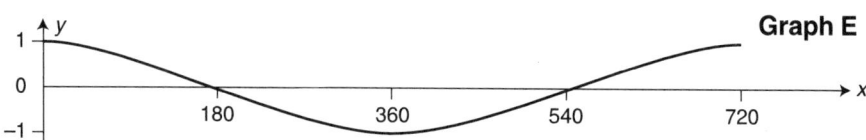

Graph E

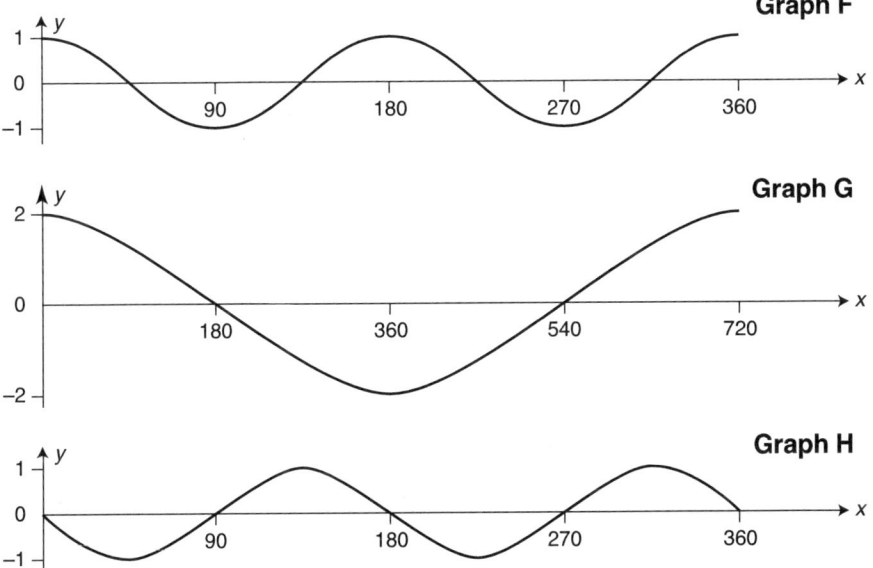

SET 61
1. Expand and simplify $(x^2 - 2)^2 - (x^2 + 2)^2$.
2. Evaluate $g(-4)$ when $g(x) = 3x^2 - 3$.
3. Simplify $\sqrt{27} + \dfrac{9}{\sqrt{3}}$.
4. $F = \dfrac{mv^2}{r}$ is a formula applicable to motion in a circle. If v and r are both doubled, what happens to F?
5. Write down the image of $(-3, -2)$ under a clockwise quarter-turn about the origin.
6. KLMN is a parallelogram with K(–2, 1), L(3, 3) and N(2, 4). Find the coordinates of M.
7. Solve the equation $3 \cos x° + 1 = 0$ where $0 \le x \le 360$.

8. Find the value of $\frac{x}{y}$.

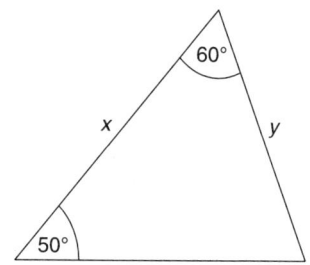

SET 62

1. Write down a formula for the perimeter of this shape.

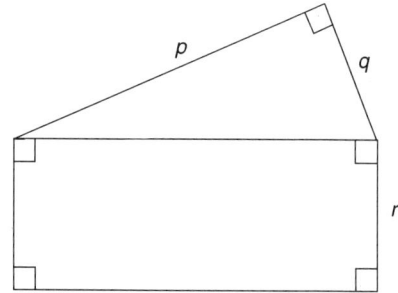

2. Factorise $6x^2 - 3xy - 3y^2$.
3. Simplify $\dfrac{a^{-1/2} \times a^2}{a^{-2}}$.
4. Sketch on plain paper the parabola $y = (x + 2)^2$.
5. Solve $3x - 2 < 4x$.
6. Calculate the value of x.

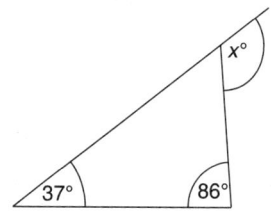

7. Calculate the size of θ, the angle subtended at the centre of a circle by an arc equal in length to the radius.

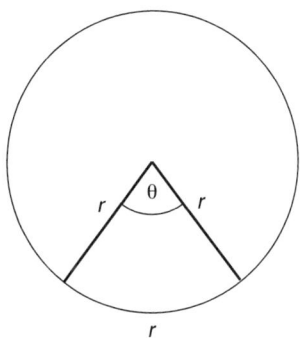

 8. Calculate the size of the largest angle of a triangle with sides 3 cm, 5 cm, 7 cm.

SET 63

1. Expand and simplify $x(2x^2 + 3x - 5) - 2(x^3 - x^2 + 2x - 3)$.
2. The shorter sides of an isosceles right-angled triangle measure $\frac{5}{\sqrt{2}}$ cm. Calculate the length of the hypotenuse.
3. Solve $x(x + 1) = 6$.
4. Make k the subject of the formula $y = \frac{k}{k-t}$.
5. How many axes of symmetry does (a) a rectangle (b) a rhombus have?
6. Find the equation of the straight line through (3, 0) and (0, −1).
7. State the cosine of the smallest angle of this triangle.

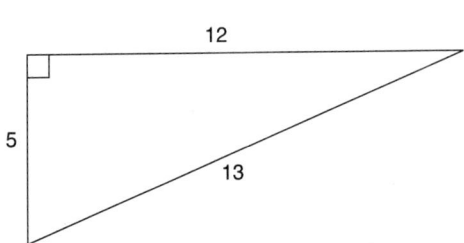

 8. ABCD is a kite with AB = BC = 5 cm, AD = DC = 6 cm, $\hat{B}$ = 41° and $\hat{D}$ = 34°. Calculate the area of the kite.

SET 64

1. Calculate the average speed of a motorist who drives for a hours at x m.p.h. and then b hours at y m.p.h.

2. Factorise fully $2a^4 - 2b^4$.

 3. A particular make of car is generally expected to lose 20% of its value during its first year, and during its second year a further 15% of its value at the start of that year. What is such a car worth now, bought for £8500 two years ago?

4. Sketch on plain paper on the same diagram the graphs of $y = x^2$ and $y = \frac{1}{2}x^2$.

5. "Every right-angled triangle has sides which are the same multiple of 3, 4, 5." Provide a counter-example to disprove this statement.

6. Calculate the area of rectangle ABCD.

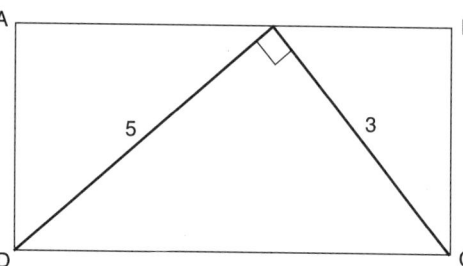

 7. Solve $5 \sin x° = -2$, $0 \leq x \leq 360$.

8. As x increases in the interval $0 < x < 180$, how does the value of $\cos x$ change?

SET 65

1. Write down the equation of the line drawn here.

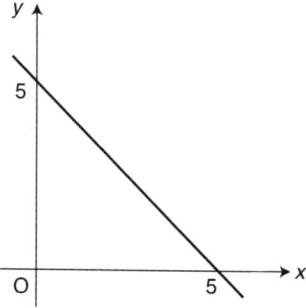

2. On plain paper, sketch the line with equation $2x + y = 4$. [Just like the figure for question 1.]

3. Write down the equation of the line drawn here.

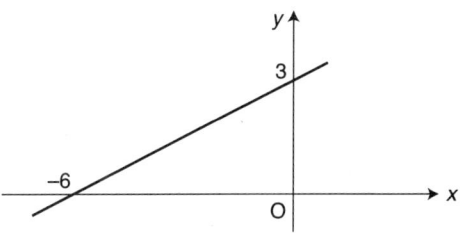

4. On plain paper, sketch the line with equation $x - 3y = 6$.

5. On plain paper, sketch the line with equation $y = 2x$.

6. State the coordinates of A and B.

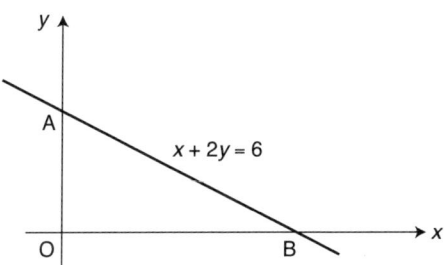

7. Find the coordinates of C.

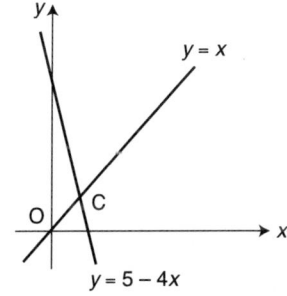

8. OABC is a rectangle. Write down the equation of
  (i) AB (ii) BC (iii) OB.

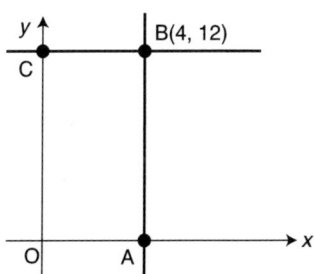

SET 66

1. Expand $(x^2 - 3)(x^2 - x - 1)$.
2. If $f(x) = 3x^2 - 2x + 1$, evaluate $f(1) - f(-1)$.
3. Calculate the standard deviation of the following set of scores from a sample:

       2   5   7   8   10   15   16

   using the formula $s = \sqrt{\dfrac{\Sigma(x - \bar{x})^2}{n - 1}}$

4. Solve $x + \dfrac{4}{x} = 5$
5. $T = 2\pi \sqrt{\dfrac{l}{g}}$ applies to the simple pendulum. In order to double T, what would have to be done to l?
6. How long is QX?

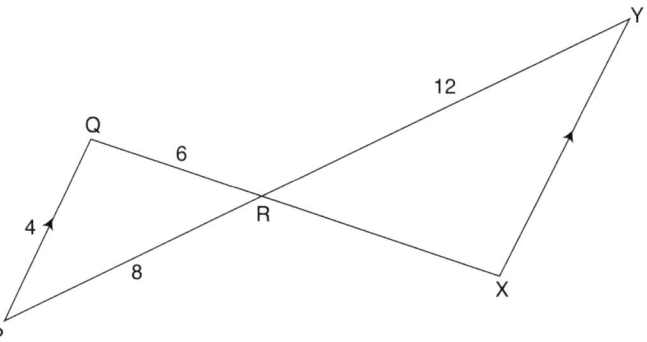

7. ABCD is a square with A(–2, –3), B(3, 0) and C(0, 5). Find the coordinates of D.
8. Find the exact value of $\tan x°$ if $\sin x° = \dfrac{5}{13}$ and $x < 90$.

SET 67

1. Evaluate $2^x b^y$ when $x = 3$, $b = 4$, $y = \frac{1}{2}$.
2. Evaluate $75 \times 9 - 15 \times 9 + 40 \times 9$.
3. Solve for x, $4^3 \times 2^{-1} = 2^x$.
4. Sketch on plain paper the parabola $y = (x - 1)^2 + 1$.
5. Solve $3x + 10 \geq 5x$ if x is a positive even number.
6. Find the ratio of the areas of triangles PST and PRQ.

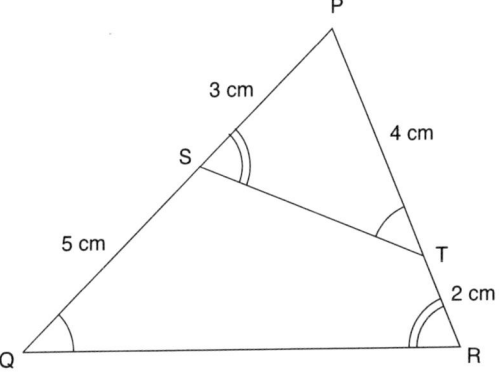

7. This is the net of a cube. When it is built up, name the point which
   (a) coincides with I,
   (b) is diagonally opposite I (2 answers).

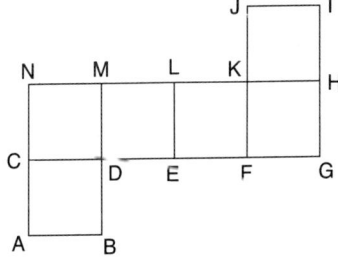

 8. Calculate the size of the smallest angle of a triangle with sides 3 cm, 5 cm and 7 cm.

SET 68

1. £100 is invested at $r\%$ compound interest (added yearly). What is the investment worth at the end of two years?
2. Factorise $9x^2 + 24xy + 16y^2$.
3. If $f(x) = x^2 - x - 1$, evaluate $f(1 + \sqrt{2})$ exactly.
4. Make v the subject of $F = \dfrac{u+v}{u-v}$.
5. If O is the centre of the circle, find x.

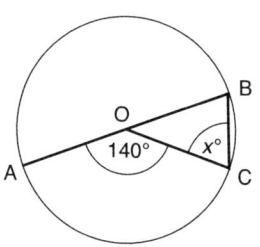

6. If the circle in question 5 has radius 30 cm, calculate the area of the sector AOC.
7. PQRS is a square. V is vertically above T. L is the mid-point of PS. Write down the tangent of angle VLT if VT = PS = 6 cm.

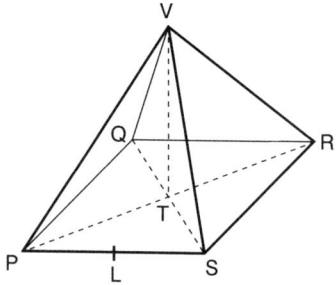

8. In triangle ABC, AB = 5 cm, BC = 6 cm. If the area of the triangle is 13·6 cm² and $A\hat{B}C$ is obtuse, calculate the size of $A\hat{B}C$.

SET 69

1. Expand and simplify $(x + 1 + a)(x + 2)$.

2. Simplify $\dfrac{2x^2 - 3x + 1}{6x^2 - 3x}$.

3. Evaluate $(9 + 16)^{1/2}$.

4. Write down the coordinates of the turning point of the graph of the parabola $y = (x+1)^2 - 1$.

5. Prove that x is a factor of 12 $\Rightarrow$ x is a factor of 24.

 6. For insurance purposes, a piece of Victorian jewellery was valued at £1500 four years ago. If jewellery has, on average, appreciated by 11% each year, what is the current value of this piece?

7. Find the equation of the straight line through $(1, 0)$ and $(0, -2)$.

8. An aeroplane flew from A to B on the bearing 063° and then from B to C on the bearing 224°. What is the size of ABC?

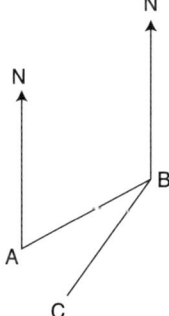

SET 70

Select the appropriate equation from equations A, B, C, D, E, F, G, H, I or J for each of these graphs. Then if you really hope to score a grade 1, you should be able to find a second equally valid answer for each from equations K, L, M, N, O, P, Q, R, S and T.

1.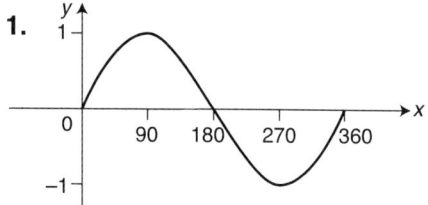

2.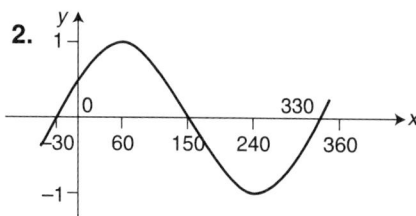

3.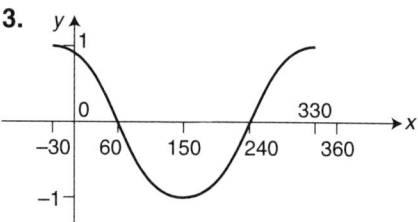

4.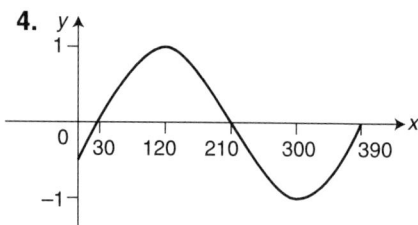

5.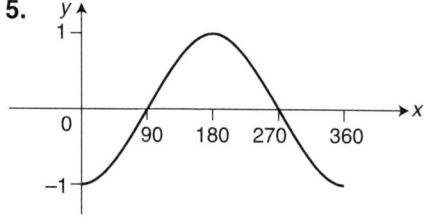

6.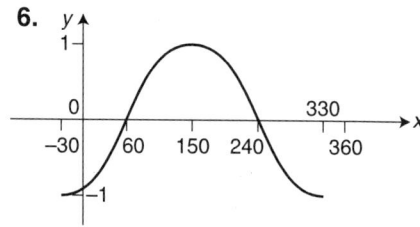

7.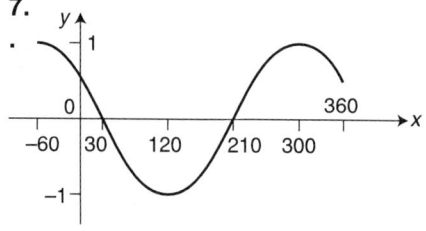

8.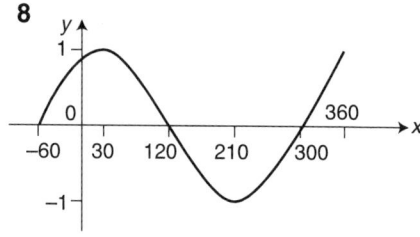

9.

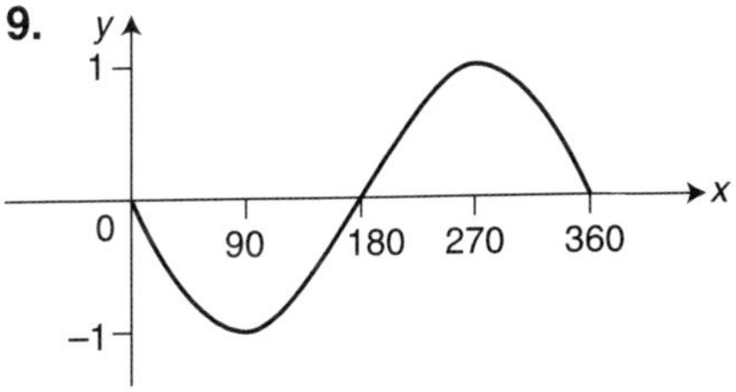

10.

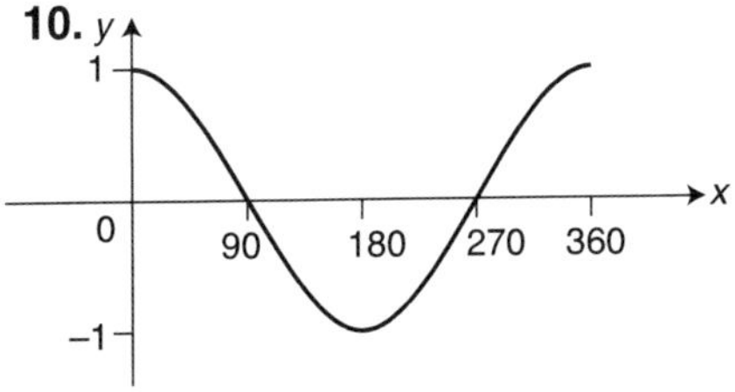

A	$y = \sin x°$	B	$y = -\sin x°$
C	$y = \sin(x + 90)°$	D	$y = \sin(x - 90)°$
E	$y = \sin(x + 30)°$	F	$y = \sin(x - 30)°$
G	$y = \sin(x + 60)°$	H	$y = \sin(x - 60)°$
I	$y = \sin(x + 120)°$	J	$y = \sin(x + 150)°$
K	$y = \cos x°$	L	$y = -\cos x°$
M	$y = \cos(x + 90)°$	N	$y = \cos(x - 90)°$
O	$y = \cos(x + 30)°$	P	$y = \cos(x - 30)°$
Q	$y = \cos(x + 60)°$	R	$y = \cos(x - 60)°$
S	$y = \cos(x - 120)°$	T	$y = \cos(x - 150)°$

SET 71

1. The "Inter City" was timed to pass ten telephone poles set 25 metres apart in 4 seconds. What was its speed in kilometres per hour?

2. Simplify $\dfrac{2-\sqrt{2}}{1+\sqrt{3}} \times \dfrac{2+\sqrt{2}}{\sqrt{3}-1}$.

3. Solve $3x(2x-1) = 0$

4. y varies as the cube of x and inversely as the square root of z. If x is trebled and z quadrupled, what happens to y?

5. What is the gradient of the line $5x - 2y = 3$?

6. *(a)* Calculate the surface area of a cuboid measuring 6 cm × 4·5 cm × 2 cm.
   (b) What would be the edge length of a cube with the same surface area?

7. Find the length of PS.

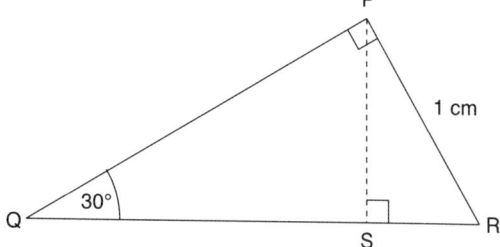

8. Solve $\cos(3x+15)° = 0$ for $0 \le x \le 90$.

SET 72

1. y varies as x^2. When $x = p$, $y = q$. Find the relationship between x and y.
2. If $g(x) = 2^n$ where $n = x^2 + x + 1$, evaluate $g(1) - g(-1)$.
3. Evaluate $a^{2/3} b^{-3/4}$ when $a = 27$ and $b = 16$.
4. Sketch on plain paper the parabola $y = 1 - (x - 1)^2$.
5. Solve $\left. \begin{array}{l} y = x + 2 \\ y = x^2 \end{array} \right\}$
6. A right-angled triangle has shorter sides 2 cm and 3 cm. A square has each side equal in length to the perimeter of the triangle. Calculate exactly the area of the square.

7. Calculate the shaded area where O is the centre of a circle radius 10 cm.

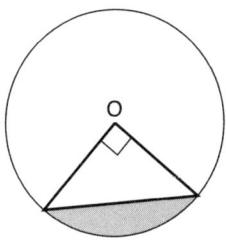

8. Solve $\tan x° = -0.6$ for $0 \leq x \leq 360$.

SET 73

1. Find the value of x^3 if $2x + 3 = -1$.
2. The line with equation $4x + y = 8$ cuts the x-axis at P and the y-axis at Q. Find the coordinates of P and Q and hence calculate the area of $\triangle OPQ$, O being the origin.
3. The hypotenuse of a right-angled triangle measures $\dfrac{2}{\sqrt{3}}$ units and is twice as long as the shortest side. Calculate exactly the length of the third side.
4. Solve $(x - 1)^2 = a^2$ for x and find the value of a if one root is twice the other.
5. Make l the subject of the formula $T = 2\pi \sqrt{\dfrac{l}{g}}$
6. If the area of triangle QRS is 4 cm², what is the area of PQRST?

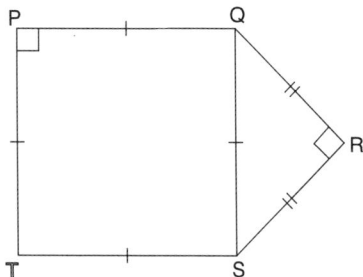

7. AT is the tangent at A to a circle with centre O and radius 5 cm. AT is 12 cm long. Calculate the length of CT.

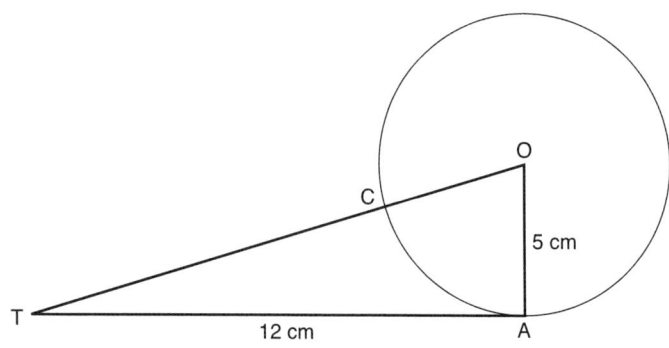

8. Calculate the size of KL̂M.

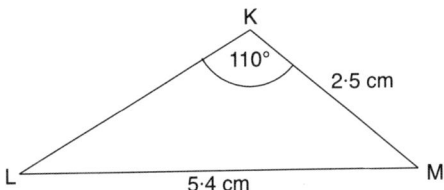

SET 74

1. Factorise fully $ab^2 - ac^2$.
2. Find $3 \times 27^{1/3} \times 81^{-3/4}$.
3. Write down the turning point of the graph of $y = (x-2)^2 + 3$.
4. Prove that the exterior angle of a triangle equals the sum of the two interior opposite angles, i.e., $a = b + c$.

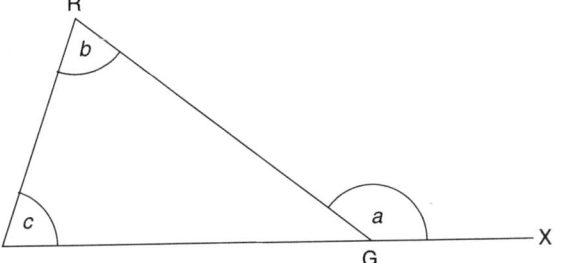

5. Calculate the area of the quadrilateral with vertices O(0, 0), A(5, 0), B(4, 7) and C(0, 9).
6. TAN is the tangent at A to the circle with centre O. Find the value of x.

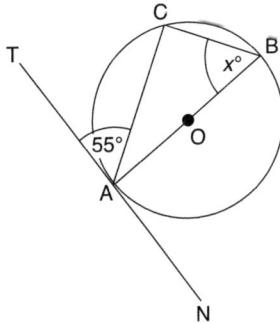

7. E, ABCD is right square pyramid with EF = 9 cm and BC = 6 cm. Find exactly the value of tan $E\hat{B}F$.

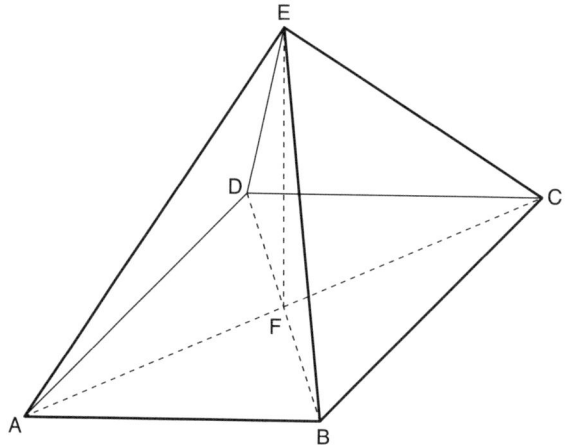

8. For $0 \le x \le 180$, when does $3 \sin 2x°$ have its maximum value and what is the maximum value?

SET 75

1. Expand $(3\sqrt{2} - \sqrt{5})^2$.
2. Solve $2(3 - x) + 3x \ge 5 - 2(1 - 2x)$.
3. Prove that the triangle with vertices $A(-1, -1)$, $B(2, 2)$ and $C(5, -1)$ is isosceles.
4. A cuboid has dimensions $3x$ cm × $2x$ cm × x cm and a cube has edge $2x$ cm. Find the ratio of their total surface areas.
5. AB, of length 24 units, is a chord of a circle of radius 13 units. Calculate the distance of AB from the centre of the circle.
6. Factorise $3 \sin^2 \theta + 13 \sin \theta - 10$.
7. If a ship sails 100 km on the bearing 220°, how far south of its starting point is it?
8. Calculate the size of $\hat{A}$.

ANSWERS

SET 1
1. $6x^2 - xy - 12y^2$
2. $(3a + 2b)(a - b)$
3. $\dfrac{3\sqrt{5}}{10}$
4. $x = -5, 9$
5. $y = \dfrac{1}{4}x^2$
6. $(-2, 11)$
7. $y = 2x - 3$
8. $209 \cdot 2$

SET 2.
1. $2x^2 - 8x + 14$
2. $\dfrac{3x^2 - 4y}{2xy}$
3. $a^{5/6}$
4. $x < 11$
5. (a) $(5, 7)$ (b) $(5, -7)$
6. $(2, 1)$
7. $y = x - 3$
8. $6 \cdot 3$ cm

SET 3
1. $16x^2 - 24xy + 9y^2$
2. $(a + 1 + b)(a + 1 - b)$
3. $2\sqrt{6}$
4. $y = \dfrac{40}{63}$
5. $b = \dfrac{1}{2}(a + 5)$
6. $(10, 1)$
7. $(-2, 0)$
8. $\dfrac{8}{17}$

SET 4
1. $3x^2 - 7xy + 2y^2$
2. 28
3. $6a^9$
4. $(2, 5)$
5. 2
6. $\sqrt{29}$
7. $2x + 3y = 0$
8. $-\cos 57°$

SET 5
1. 6
2. $\dfrac{29}{36}$
3. 50p
4. $3\dfrac{1}{4}$ h
5. $44 \cdot 4\%$
6. 20
7. 26th September
8. 6

SET 6
1. $2(2x - 3y)(2x + 3y)$
2. $\dfrac{4\sqrt{3}}{3}$
3. $x = -1\dfrac{1}{2}, 3$
4. $x = \dfrac{y^2}{2\sqrt{z}}$
5. (a) No (b) No
6. $255°$
7. $7 \cdot 85$
8. $3 \cdot 7$ cm

SET 7
1. −19
2. $\dfrac{4b-3a}{2ab}$
3. $\dfrac{3}{8}$
4. $x = 1$
5. $x < 3$
6. $\sqrt{3}$ m
7. $\dfrac{2}{3}$
8. $\dfrac{k+4}{k+6}$

SET 8
1. $6x^2 + 11xy - 10y^2$
2. $\sqrt{2}$
3. $x = 18$
4. $q = \dfrac{1}{3}(2p - y)$
5. False
6. (10, 6)
7. $x + y = 5$
8. $\theta = 115 \cdot 5°$

SET 9
1. $25x^2 - 30xy + 9y^2$
2. a
3. $(3, -7)$
4. n is either even or odd,
   if n is even, then $n(n + 1)$ is even,
   if n is odd, then $(n + 1)$ is even, so $n(n + 1)$ is even.
5. $x = 3, y = 1\dfrac{1}{3}$
6. 9·8 m
7. (1·5, 0)
8.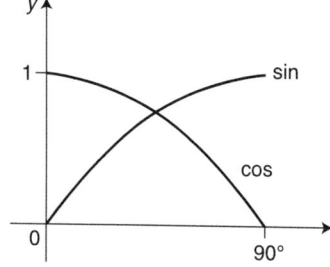

SET 10
1. 7
2. $6 \cdot 74 \times 10^{-3}$
3. $\dfrac{3}{14}$
4. £25.20
5. 12
6. £500
7. 44%
8. (a) $\dfrac{1}{2}$ (b) $\dfrac{1}{13}$ (c) $\dfrac{1}{26}$

SET 11
1. $-2a + 27c + 8d$
2. $2\sqrt{3}$
3. $x = -38$
4. $p = 20$
5. 28 cm
6. $\left(5\frac{1}{2}, 7\right)$
7. $2y = 3x$
8. $\frac{5}{13}$

SET 12
1. $x^2 + 4y^2$
2. $(a + b + 2c)(a + b - 2c)$
3. $\frac{1}{a}$
4. $(3, 5)$
5. $x = 4, y = 2$
6. $242°$
7. Rectangle
8. $70{\cdot}5, 289{\cdot}5$

SET 13
1. $4x^2 + 12xy + 9y^2$
2. $\frac{2a^2 + b^2}{2ab}$
3. $\frac{\sqrt{2}}{2}$
4. $r = \frac{1}{4}(3 - h)$
5. $(5, 8)$
6. RQ by 2 units
7. $\frac{1}{5}$
8. $34{\cdot}0°$

SET 14
1. -201
2. a^3
3. $x = 3$
4. (a) $(3, 5)$ (b) $(-3, 5)$
5. $(4, -1)$
6. $3x - y = 0$
7. $\tan \theta = \frac{7}{24}$
8. $0, 180, 360$

SET 15
1. 27
2. $0{\cdot}009$
3. 7 cm
4. 110 h
5. 44 km / h
6. $\frac{1}{6}$
7. 65
8. e.g., $2x + y = 6; 2$

SET 16
1. 23
2. $9 + 4\sqrt{2}$
3. $y = 1\frac{1}{5}$
4. $q = 16$
5. $(7, 0)$
6. $5\sqrt{5}$
7. $y = 2x$
8. $\frac{g}{\sin G} = \frac{h}{\sin H} = \frac{k}{\sin K}$

SET 17
1. $(5x-y)(x+2y)$
2. $x=3$
3. $x \geq 1\frac{1}{2}$
4. 12 cm^2
5. 10
6. $(-2, 0)$
7. 270
8. $9\frac{1}{2}$ feet

SET 18
1. $2a^2 + 2b^2$
2. $\frac{2x+1}{x}$
3. $-9, 1$
4. $\frac{a-b}{s}$
5. $130°$
6. $330°$
7. $y = 2x - 1$
8. 35

SET 19
1. $49x^2 - 14y + y^2$
2. $(a-b-c)(a-b+c)$
3. 1
4. Let n be an odd integer
   $\Rightarrow n = 2x + 1$
   $\Rightarrow n^2 = (2x+1)^2 = 4x^2 + 4x + 1 = 4(x^2 + x) + 1$
   $\Rightarrow n^2$ has remainder 1 when divided by 4
5. $5\sqrt{2}$ cm
6. $130°$
7. $127.6°$
8. (a) 1 (b) 2

SET 20
1. 8.3×10^7
2. $\frac{2}{3}$
3. £27.75
4. 4
5. 48 km/h
6. £6.50
7. 5%
8. $\frac{1}{4}$

SET 21
1. $6x^2 + 5xy - 6y^2$
2. 8
3. $\frac{\sqrt{2}}{10}$
4. $x = 2, 3$
5. $y = 2\sqrt[3]{x}$
6. $x = 14$
7. $\frac{-3}{4}$
8. 9.4 m

SET 22
1. 38
2. 125
3. $3(r-p)$
4. $8 : 27$
5. $t\sqrt{2}$
6. $(4, 0)$
7. 0.7
8. $p^2 = q^2 + r^2 - 2qr \cos P$

SET 23
1. $5a^3 + 7b^2$ 2. $(3x-1)(2x+9)$ 3. $3\sqrt{2}$ 4. $x = -2, 1$
5. $x < 1\frac{2}{3}$ 6. 10   7. $x + 3y = 0$ 8. 57·7

SET 24
1. $9x^2 + 6xy + y^2$ 2. $\frac{x-1}{x}$ 3. $16\frac{1}{2}$ 4. $(-2, -6)$
5. $n^3 - n = n(n^2 - 1) = n(n-1)(n+1) = (n-1)n(n+1)$
This is the product of three consecutive integers so one is a multiple of 3 and either n is or $(n-1)$, $(n+1)$ are even hence $n^3 - n$ is divisible by 2 and 3, thus 6 is a factor $n^3 - n$.
6. 180   7. $4\frac{8}{9}$ m   8. (a) $y = -2$ (b) $x = 3$ (c) $2x + 3y = 0$

SET 25
1. 11   2. $3\frac{1}{3}$ 3. £2.42   4. 94 cm^2
5. 42 m.p.h.   6. £103.84   7. 59   8. 1

SET 26
1. $4x^2 - 4xy + y^2$ 2. $(3x-1)(2x-1)$ 3. $\frac{3\sqrt{7}}{7}$
4. $(x, y) = (4, -1)$ 5. $y = \frac{k\sqrt{x}}{z}$ 6. $\frac{2}{3}$
7. $\frac{12}{5}$ 8. $\frac{5 \sin 60°}{\sin 70°}$

SET 27
1. $P = 6x + 8$ 2. 27   3. minimum   4. $(2, -3)$
5. $(-2, 1)$ 6. $(0, 3)$ 7. 14·5, 165·5   8. $\cos S = \frac{r^2 + t^2 - s^2}{2rt}$

SET 28
1. 5000   2. $\sqrt{2}$ 3. $x = \pm 3$ 4. $h = \frac{3V}{\pi r^2}$
5. 17·5 cm^2 6. $PY = 13$ cm   7. $\frac{-3}{2}$ 8. 13·5 cm^2

SET 29

1. $\dfrac{5p^2 - 4q}{2pq}$
2. $a^{11/12}$
3. $x = 4\dfrac{1}{2}$
4. If $\triangle ABC$ is isosceles with $AB = AC$, then the perpendicular bisector of BC is both the median and the altitude through A.

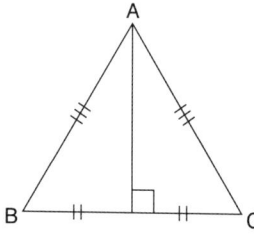

5. $90°$
6. $(3, 8)$
7. $k = -7$
8. $-\sin 68°$

SET 30

1. 25
2. 4×10^7
3. 20 min
4. 209·95
5. 7p
6. £66
7. £4400
8. 1,1 1,2 1,3 1,4 1,5 1,6 ; $\dfrac{5}{12}$
   2,1 2,2 2,3 2,4 2,5 2,6
   3,1 3,2 3,3 3,4 3,5 3,6
   4,1 4,2 4,3 4,4 4,5 4,6
   5,1 5,2 5,3 5,4 5,5 5,6
   6,1 6,2 6,3 6,4 6,5 6,6

SET 31

1. $(3a + b)(2a - b)$
2. $\dfrac{3\sqrt{2}}{5}$
3. $-3, -1$
4. $x = \dfrac{k\sqrt{y}}{z^3}$
5. $032°$
6. 2·5
7. $x = 124, 236$
8. $53·1°$

SET 32

1. $9x^2y^2 - 42xyz + 49z^2$
2. 3
3. 9
4. 6
5. $OP = 25$ mm, $OQ = 35$ mm
6. $4\sqrt{2}$
7. 116·6, 296·6
8. 76

SET 33

1. $\pi(x - y)(x + y)$
2. $\dfrac{3\sqrt{10}}{20}$
3. $0·5, -2·1$
4. $k = \dfrac{1}{2}(p + 2q)$
5. $x = 2\dfrac{1}{2}$
6. (a) $(-1, 5)$ (b) 10
7. $2x + 3y = 2$
8. $\dfrac{15}{17}$

SET 34
1. $6a^2 - 7ab - 3b^2$
2. $(3x+2)(4x-3)$
3. $x = 4$
4. $x = -4$
5. $\cos \theta° = \dfrac{x}{r}$
   $\theta + \phi = 90$
   $\Rightarrow \phi = 90 - \theta$
   $\Rightarrow \sin(90 - \theta)° = \sin \phi°$
   $\quad\quad\quad\quad = \dfrac{x}{r} = \cos \theta°$

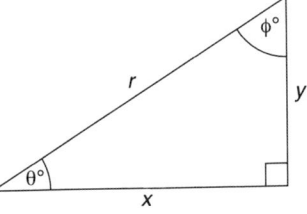

6. $\left(1\tfrac{1}{4}, 0\right)$
7. 123·6, 303·6
8. 36

SET 35
1. (2, 0)
2. (0, −3)
3. 3 units²
4. $\dfrac{3}{2}$
5. $\sqrt{13}$
6. $\dfrac{6}{\sqrt{13}}$
7. $3x = 2y$
8. $3x - 2y = 2$

SET 36
1. $2a - 2b$
2. $\dfrac{x+1}{x}$
3. $\dfrac{2}{7}$
4. $x = \dfrac{-1}{3}, \dfrac{1}{2}$
5. $\left(0, -\dfrac{1}{2}\right)$
6. 225°
7. £324
8. 5·08

SET 37
1. $(xy - 3)(xy + 3)$
2. $\dfrac{2}{3}$
3. (0, 4)
4. $x > 1$
5. (2, −1)
6. 22 cm²
7. $\dfrac{\sqrt{2}}{2}$
8. $\dfrac{q^2 + r^2 - p^2}{2qr}$

SET 38
1. 12
2. $\dfrac{1}{3}$
3. $x = \dfrac{-b \pm \sqrt{b^2 - 4ac}}{2a}$
4. $r = \sqrt{\dfrac{A}{4\pi}}$
5. (3, 4)
6. 070°
7. $\dfrac{1}{2}$
8. 0·7

SET 39
1. $6a^2 + ab - 2b^2$
2. $(2x-1)(x-1)$
3. $\frac{1}{81}$
4. $x = 2$ [$x = h$, for any h]
5. 10 units^2
6. $-\frac{1}{4}$
7. $y = 2x + 4$
8. [graph of sine-like curve through 0, 180, 360 on x-axis, amplitude 1]

SET 40
1. 5
2. $\left(-\frac{1}{2}, 1\right)$
3. $2x + y = 0$
4. $\frac{-4}{3}$
5. $(4, -5)$
6. $(3, -2)$
7. $(1, -1)$
8. $45°$

SET 41
1. $16x - 5y$
2. $\frac{x-1}{x-2}$
3. $\frac{2\sqrt{5}}{15}$
4. $x = -4, 1$
5. 1
6. $3y + 2x = 0$
7. $\frac{4}{5}$
8. $11\cdot1$

SET 42
1. £160
2. $3(x - 3y)(x + 3y)$
3. $x = -2$
4. $(3, -6)$
5. 6 units^2
6. $y = 3, x = 5$
7. $109\cdot5, 250\cdot5$
8. $\frac{1}{4}$

SET 43
1. $7y^2 - xy - x^2$
2. -3
3. $6\sqrt{2}$
4. $x = \frac{y-b}{a}$
5. $x = 5\frac{1}{3}, y = 3\frac{3}{4}$
6. $335°$
7. $34°$
8. 5

SET 44
1. 100
2. $\frac{1}{b^5}$ (or b^{-5})
3. $(2, 16)$
4. e.g., $x^2 + 4x + 4 = 0 \Rightarrow (x+2)^2 = 0 \Rightarrow x = -2, -2$
5. $4:9$
6. $y = -5x + 5$
7. $0\cdot8$
8. $\frac{-2}{3}$

SET 45
1. 30° 2. 47·1 cm² 3. 9 cm² 4. 22·4 cm
5. −3, 5 6. $x = 1$ 7. −16 8. (0, −15)

SET 46
1. $62x^2m^2$ 2. 0·290, −0·690 3. 4 4. (−5, 12)
5. −1 6. $y = 2x + 5$ 7. $x = 122·8, 237·2$ 8. e.g., $y = 3x − 2$; 4

SET 47
1. The former is better by 96 p   2. $\dfrac{2y + x}{y}$ 3. $\dfrac{1}{16}$
4. 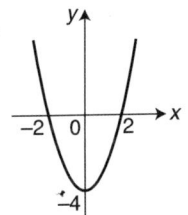   5. $x \leq 1$ 6. (−2, 5)
7. (2, −2)   8. 9 units²

SET 48
1. $10x^2 − 7xy − 12y^2$ 2. $(3x + 2)(2x − 3)$ 3. 12 cm² 4. $x = \dfrac{1}{8}$
5. $r = \dfrac{100I}{Pn}$ 6. $k = 3$ 7. $\dfrac{4}{5}$ 8. 16·1 cm²

SET 49
1. $\dfrac{63}{64}$ 2. (2, 5)
3. Let x be any even number   4. (−5, 3)
   then $x = 2y$
   $\Rightarrow x^2 = 4y^2 \Rightarrow$ the square is divisible by 4
5.    6. 20°   7. $\dfrac{1}{6}$ 8.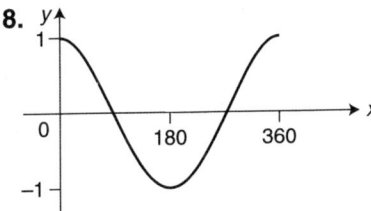

SET 50
1. E 2. A 3. J 4. I 5. G
6. B 7. H 8. C 9. D 10. F

SET 51
1. $3x^2 + 5xy - 2y^2$
2. $(x-2)(x+2)(x^2+4)$
3. $6\sqrt{5}$
4. $x = 2\frac{5}{8}$
5. Multiply by 8
6. 24 cm^2
7. $y = 3x + 9$

8.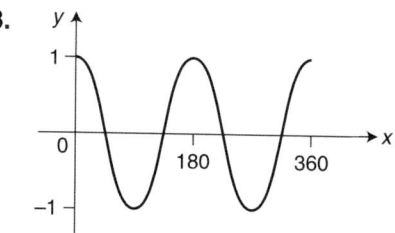

SET 52
1. $\dfrac{x-2}{2(x-3)}$
2. p^4
3.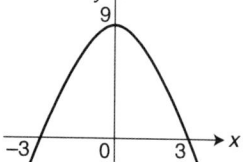
4. $x < 2$
5. (a) 0, (b) 4
6. $(7, 7)$
7. $y = \dfrac{1}{5}x - 1$ or $x - 5y = 5$
8. 3.44 cm

SET 53
1. 10
2. $3(x-1)^2$
3. $4\sqrt{2}$
4. $x = -3, 2$
5. (a) 2, (b) 4
6. (a) 216 cm^3, (b) 6 cm
7. $x = 110, 250$
8.  $\dfrac{\sin x°}{\sin y°}$

SET 54
1. $a^2 + ab - ac - 2b^2 + bc$
2. $-5\frac{1}{2}$
3. $\dfrac{1}{81}$
4.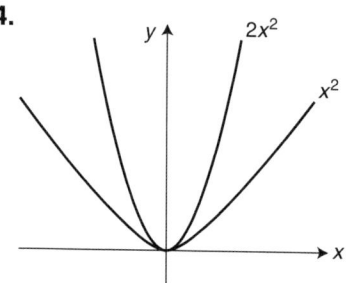
5. 2.25 m
6. $(a, 0)$
7. $r = -1$
8. $2 \sin a°$

SET 55
1. D 2. C 3. A 4. B 5. (i) 20, (ii) 5
6. (i) 20, (ii) 1 7. 20 8. 1·26

SET 56
1. $10x^2 + 5xy$ 2. $x(x-2)(x+2)$ 3. $\dfrac{\sqrt{2}}{3}$ 4. 6 cm
5. 150° 6. 23·6 cm 7. 35° 8. 9·1

SET 57
1. $10x^2 + 29xy - 21y^2$ 2. $(3\cos x° + 1)(\cos x° - 1)$ 3. $\dfrac{1}{8}$
4. 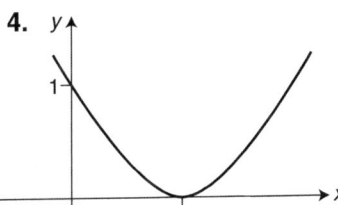   5. $x = 8, y = 1$ 6. 12 units
7. $y = -\dfrac{1}{2}x + 1$ or $x + 2y - 2 = 0$
8. 104·3°

SET 58
1. $2xy - 2xz$ or $2x(y-z)$ 2. $\dfrac{9p^2 - 16q^2}{12pq}$ 3. $4\sqrt{2}$
4. $x = 2\cdot1$ 5. $c = \dfrac{b}{W+1}$ 6. $(-4, 10)$ 7. 34·1 units^2
8. 1,1 1,2 1,3 1,4 1,5 ; $\dfrac{1}{5}$
   2,1 2,2 2,3 2,4 2,5
   3,1 3,2 3,3 3,4 3,5
   4,1 4,2 4,3 4,4 4,5
   5,1 5,2 5,3 5,4 5,5

SET 59
1. $5(x - 2y^2)(x + 2y^2)$ 2. -1 3.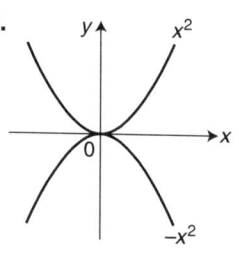
4. $n = 4$ or 5 5. 5
6. 18 7. $\dfrac{3}{5}$

8.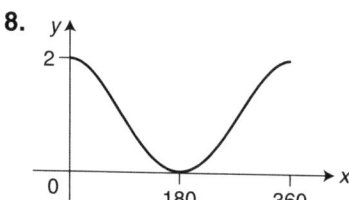

SET 60
1. B   2. F   3. C   4. D   5. A   6. E   7. H   8. G

SET 61
1. $-8x^2$ 2. 45 3. $6\sqrt{3}$ 4. Doubled   5. $(-2, 3)$
6. $(7, 6)$ 7. $109\cdot5, 250\cdot5$ 8. $\dfrac{\sin 70°}{\sin 50°} = 1\cdot23$

SET 62
1. $p + q + 2r + \sqrt{p^2 + q^2}$ 2. $3(2x + y)(x - y)$ 3. $a^{7/2}$
4. 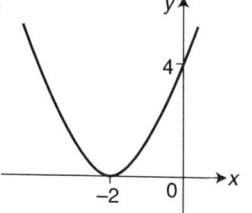   5. $x > -2$
6. 123
7. $57\cdot3°$
8. $120°$

SET 63
1. $5x^2 - 9x + 6$ 2. 5 3. $x = -3, 2$ 4. $k = \dfrac{yt}{y - 1}$
5. (a) 2, (b) 2 6. $y = \dfrac{1}{3}x - 1$ or $x - 3y - 3 = 0$
7. $\dfrac{12}{13}$ 8. $18\cdot3$ cm^2

SET 64

1. $\dfrac{ax+by}{a+b}$

2. $2(a-b)(a+b)(a^2+b^2)$

3. £5780

4.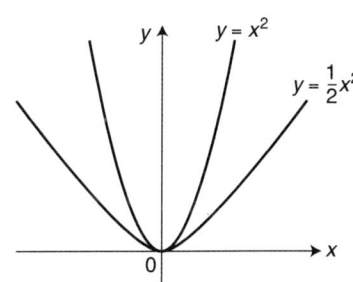

5. e.g., a 5, 12,13 △
6. 15 units^2
7. $x = 203 \cdot 6, 336 \cdot 4$
8. decreases continuously

SET 65

1. $x + y = 5$
2.
3. $y = \dfrac{1}{2}x + 3$ or $x - 2y + 6 = 0$

4.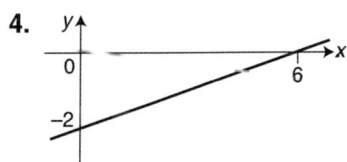
5.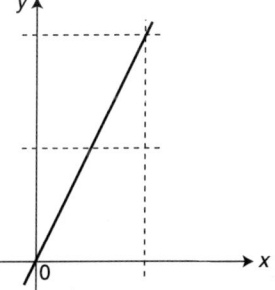

6. A(0, 3), B(6, 0)
7. (1, 1)
8. (i) $x = 4$, (ii) $y = 12$, (iii) $y = 3x$

SET 66

1. $x^4 - x^3 - 4x^2 + 3x + 3$
2. -4
3. $5 \cdot 10$
4. $x = 1, 4$
5. multiply by 4
6. 15
7. (−5, 2)
8. $\dfrac{5}{12}$

SET 67
1. 16
2. 900
3. $x = 5$
4.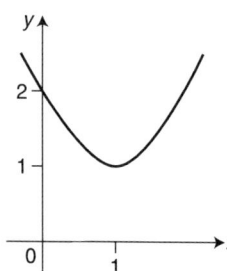
5. $x = 2, 4$
6. $1 : 4$
7. (a) M, (b) F, A
8. $21 \cdot 8°$

SET 68
1. $\dfrac{(100 + r)^2}{100}$ or $100 + 2r + \dfrac{r^2}{100}$
2. $(3x + 4y)^2$
3. $1 + \sqrt{2}$
4. $\dfrac{(F - 1)u}{F + 1}$
5. 70
6. 1100 cm^2
7. 2
8. $115°$

SET 69
1. $x^2 + (a + 3)x + (2a + 2)$
2. $\dfrac{x - 1}{3x}$
3. 5
4. $(-1, -1)$
5. x is a factor of $12 \Rightarrow 12 = x \cdot y$
   $\Rightarrow 24 = 2 \times 12$
   $= 2 \cdot x \cdot y = x(2y)$
   $\Rightarrow x$ is a factor of 24
6. £2277
7. $y = 2x - 2$
8. $19°$

SET 70
1. A or N
2. E or R
3. I or O
4. F or S
5. D or L
6. H or T
7. J or Q
8. G or P
9. B or M
10. C or K

SET 71
1. $202 \cdot 5$ km / h
2. 1
3. $x = 0, \dfrac{1}{2}$
4. Multiplied by $\dfrac{27}{2}$
5. $\dfrac{5}{2}$
6. (a) 96 cm^2, (b) 4 cm
7. $\dfrac{\sqrt{3}}{2} = 0 \cdot 866$
8. $x = 25, 85$

SET 72

1. $y = \dfrac{qx^2}{p^2}$
2. 6
3. $\dfrac{9}{8}$
4.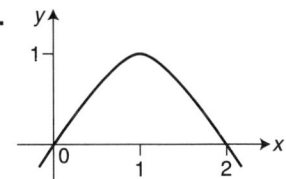
5. $(x, y) = (-1, 1), (2, 4)$
6. $38 + 10\sqrt{13}$
7. 28.5 cm^2
8. $x = 149.0, 329.0$

SET 73

1. -8
2. $P(2, 0), Q(0, 8), 8$ units^2
3. 1 unit
4. $x = 1 \pm a, \ a = \dfrac{1}{3}$
5. $l = \dfrac{T^2 g}{4\pi^2}$
6. 20 cm^2
7. 8 cm
8. $25.8°$

SET 74

1. $a(b - c)(b + c)$
2. $\dfrac{1}{3}$
3. $(2, 3)$
4. Let $R\hat{G}F = d$
   $\Rightarrow a + d = 180°$ and $b + c + d = 180°$
   $\Rightarrow a = b + c$ (both equal $180° - d$)
5. $35\dfrac{1}{2}$ units^2
6. 55
7. $\dfrac{3\sqrt{2}}{2}$
8. $x = 45°, 3$

SET 75

1. $23 - 6\sqrt{10}$
2. $x \leq 1$
3. $AB = BC$
4. $11 : 12$
5. 5 units
6. $(3 \sin \theta - 2)(\sin \theta + 5)$
7. 76.6 km
8. $120°$

RECORD YOUR PROGRESS ON THIS CHART

Date	Set	Score	Date	Set	Score	Date	Set	Score
	1			26			51	
	2			27			52	
	3			28			53	
	4			29			54	
	5			30			55	
	6			31			56	
	7			32			57	
	8			33			58	
	9			34			59	
	10			35			60	
	11			36			61	
	12			37			62	
	13			38			63	
	14			39			64	
	15			40			65	
	16			41			66	
	17			42			67	
	18			43			68	
	19			44			69	
	20			45			70	
	21			46			71	
	22			47			72	
	23			48			73	
	24			49			74	
	25			50			75	

Printed by Bell & Bain Ltd., Glasgow, Scotland, U.K.